PERSUADE

Nick Baldock was an international speaker and sales improvement consultant. He had a highly successful sales career which spanned three industries—finance, media advertising and recruitment. From 1985, Nick delighted audiences across Europe and the USA as a motivational speaker, sales trainer and business development consultant. Organisations such as the Royal Bank of Scotland, British Airways and BMW have testified to the value of his skills and experience.

Nick published his first book, *Running across America*, in 2000 and his second book, *The Value House* in 2011. Not long after completing his third book, *Persuade*, he passed away on 12 July 2014.

Bob Hayward is a Christian and a father of four, as well as a director of three companies including Be More Effective Ltd, a business growth and employee engagement consultancy. He built five businesses he started to £1M turnover or more. He has a raft of practical knowledge and experience that make him a natural and informative speaker with a complete understanding of the needs of employees and problems facing business owners and managers.

Bob has designed and delivered numerous internal communication and employee engagement projects for companies like Vodafone, Peugeot, and Somerfield, and has run many skill development programmes. He is a highly-experienced consultant, facilitator, trainer and speaker.

PERSUADE

How to Persuade Anyone about Anything

NICK BALDOCK AND
BOB HAYWARD

RUPA

Published by
Rupa Publications India Pvt. Ltd 2025
7/16, Ansari Road, Daryaganj
New Delhi 110002

Sales centres:
Bengaluru Chennai
Hyderabad Jaipur Kathmandu
Kolkata Mumbai Prayagraj

Copyright © Nick Baldock and Bob Hayward 2025
This edition of *Persuade: How to Persuade Anyone about Anything* is published by arrangement with Rethink Press.

The views and opinions expressed in this book are the authors' own and the facts are as reported by them which have been verified to the extent possible, and the publishers are not in any way liable for the same.

All rights reserved.
No part of this publication may be reproduced, transmitted, or stored in a retrieval system, in any form or by any means, electronic, mechanical, photocopying, recording or otherwise, without the prior permission of the publisher.

P-ISBN: 978-93-5702-691-8
E-ISBN: 978-93-5702-951-3

First impression 2025

10 9 8 7 6 5 4 3 2 1

The moral right of the authors has been asserted.

Printed in India

This book is sold subject to the condition that it shall not, by way of trade or otherwise, be lent, resold, hired out, or otherwise circulated, without the publisher's prior consent, in any form of binding or cover other than that in which it is published.

Contents

Introduction   *vii*

1. Context   1
2. The Basis of Persuasion   23
3. Persuade—The Model   47
4. Other Factors That Persuade   113
5. Famous and Infamous Stories of Persuasion   146
6. Case Studies and Applications   188
7. The Summary   230

Introduction

Why would you want to persuade anyone about anything?

Let's face it, there are times when most of us would have to admit that despite our willingness to get on with others, we do desire to have things our own way. It may not be possible to always have things go the way we would prefer by themselves, and so the reality is that influencing skills are indispensable in many modern life and work situations.

- Do you lead, manage, or supervise others?
- Do you find it a challenge to get everything you need from suppliers, sub-contractors or colleagues?
- Would you like to increase sales from your advertising or marketing?
- Maybe you find getting your ideas across effectively in meetings a challenge?
- Nobody ever poses an objection to your ideas or proposals, do they?
- Would you like to be more confident and persuasive?

To fulfil our ambitions, to build a business or career, to win or complete a project successfully or bring up a family well—all these things either happen or don't because of our ability to bring others with us, to cause them to buy into our ideas. Persuasion is a skill—part psychology, part human relationships, part communication. Can you turn people around, so others see things your way all the time? Probably not; but what we can all do is increase our success rate so that more people, more often, willingly go along with our ideas.

Now if you are thinking persuasion is just not you... be careful. I don't suppose as a baby you ever cried for food, or as a teenager stomped, sulked or whined until you got your way? No, of course you didn't. And you didn't whisper sweet nothings into the ear of that boy or girl you fancied to secure a date? No, of course not...

That accepted—you might want to consider this book a support to you in case you ever have to persuade someone in the future. If you have ambitions, big or small, long term or immediate, the chances are you will want to persuade someone, sometime, to your way of thinking.

Before we go too far, it might be best to agree a definition of our topic—Persuasion.

Persuade means

According to a variety of dictionaries the word persuade means the following:

- To cause someone or convince them to do or to believe something by various means including giving them a good reason to do it or believe it
- To induce, urge or prevail upon another to undertake a course of action or embrace a point of view by means of argument, reasoning or entreaty
- To prevail on a person to do something, as by influencing, advising or urging

Introduction

There is a variety of other words and phrases that are closely associated with our chosen word 'persuade', such as:

- To win approval or support for, to sway, to carry
- To influence, act upon, tempt or charm
- To induce into action
- To twist somebody's arm
- To hustle—pressure or urge someone into an action
- To bring around or turn around
- To cause to adopt an opinion or course of action, new or different from what preceded it
- To badger through constant efforts
- To sell to somebody such that they accept something
- To chat up someone with the aim of getting your way
- To talk someone into something
- To rope in—draw in as if with a rope or lure
- To cajole, coax, inveigle, sweet-talk, wheedle, caress or flatter
- To convince, win over, convert
- To make someone agree, understand, or realise the truth or validity of something
- To brainwash
- To induce, stimulate, create, get, have—cause to do, or cause to act in a specified manner
- To assure

You can see that not every phrase or word associated with persuading is wholly positive or complimentary about the person doing the persuading.

Persuasion does get a bad press at times. In the land of the unsavoury person, the high-pressure/low-ethical, fast-buck, me-me-me culture, you are likely to find that manipulative subliminal techniques and shameless ploys are all acceptable tools of the trade.

There have been plenty of political leaders, business executives, journalists and tradesmen that have used a deftly chosen compliment, a kind of smile, gesture or phrase to get their way. A silvery tongue can lead millions to follow an immoral cause just because the approach appears reassuring and soft, but it does not mean the intention is reasonable and fair.

Does that mean that persuasion is bad? No—it means that if someone's intentions are less than honourable, then whatever tactic they use or outcome they achieve will be tainted by their negative or selfish intention. The 'badness' is in the intention and not in the tool itself. Any form of human interaction is turned by the intention of those involved in either a good or bad exercise, to fulfil either honourable or destructive ambitions.

This book on persuasion is written with sound intentions: that this skill of persuasion, this approach to persuade others, when used with integrity for genuinely positive outcomes for all involved produces a much better result. It has been said that one volunteer is worth that of nine pressed men, a throwback to the days when men were forced to work on sailing ships. They were persuaded by clubs, knives and guns by what were known as 'Press Gangs'. By improving our understanding of and skill at persuasion, our aim is that you will more often be able to secure the 'willing support' of those around you. Effective persuasion wins the heart and mind so that you almost have a volunteer on your hands.

Is persuade just another term for influencing, selling or negotiation?

In many ways yes, 'persuade' is a similar term, because...

- Negotiation is a mutual discussion or process about the arrangement of the terms of a transaction or agreement; it is an activity that people use to influence others. To persuade someone, we must go through a process even if it only involves one conversation. Influence is the power to affect a person, thing or course of events without apparent exertion of force or the direct exercise of command. And to efficiently persuade we must influence. If you force an alternative view on another—they are of the same opinion still; you have a resistant mind on your hands, and that reluctance will cost you dearly regarding time, effort or money. In the worse cases, it will cost you all three!
- Selling means at least these two things:
  1. To cause something to be accepted; to advocate or promote the worth or desirability of a course of action successfully.
  2. To give up (a house, some money or a point of view) to another for (or in return for) something of value.

To effectively persuade, generally we must put across our ideas well enough for others to find them attractive. That means the other person must see something significant or of genuine value in them. Often, when persuading, we must get others to give up their previously-held position. Some new position tends to be replacing some old; most people have an opinion or default bias on things in life, so you rarely win a blank canvas to work with or a vacuum to operate in. They already hold a view or an opinion about the topic in question, and this is in place at the start of our interaction with them. For our target to accept a new option or our idea, we must somehow cause that original point of view to be given up.

In some ways no, 'persuade' is not a similar term, because…

In sales and negotiation at least, there is a trade going on. To put it at its simplest level in sales, I have a product you might want, and you have some cash that I might want—so we trade. With negotiation the trade is different; it is more like the story of two children and one orange. They cannot both have the whole orange, but one child wants the flesh to squeeze into orange juice, and the other wants the skin or pith to add as an ingredient to the cake she wishes to make. If they negotiate effectively, they can have everything they really want. One can have all the orange peel, and the other can have all the flesh. In both situations, there is some trading going on. There is dialogue, there is understanding or appreciation of the value, and there is a trade.

With persuasion, there is no trade. I see something this way—you see it that way, and somehow, I must get you to accept the way I see it. There is no trade. We are not swapping ideas or goods, and I am not giving up my position to take up yours; I must persuade you to join me on my side of the fence.

Unfortunately, this type of influencing or persuasion can often be thought of as wrong. It is often portrayed in the media as manipulation; whether that is the politician putting a 'spin' on an issue to turn a negative situation to their advantage (often perceived as dishonest exaggeration at best, and lying at its worst) or whether that is the advertising at Christmas which positions only those parents as good if they buy presents from a particular store or catalogue. Of course, that infers that those parents who do not are bad.

Manipulation is an act where a person is led towards something that is not in their best interest by controlling, confusing or subverting their natural thought process. The manipulator is going to get what he or she wants at the other's expense. If you are on the other end of manipulation, in many ways you are being psychologically abused; with manipulation, there is an adversarial and dishonest covert deception going on. Someone is doing something to you and without you even knowing it at the time.

Persuasion happens in the open, it engages all parties reasonably and consciously; their thinking, their emotions and their behaviour. It is a strategy or at least a process that is meant to solve a problem, to resolve a difference and ultimately to benefit everyone involved. Persuasion is the process of guiding people toward the adoption of a new or different idea, attitude or action by dialogue or interaction—willingly and without duress or pressure.

What is the purpose of this book?

So, you get the point—the focus of our attention—the central theme of this book is persuasion. But why write another book on this topic; after all, it is not as if this book is the first one on persuasion?

For fun, type 'books on persuasion' into your favourite search engine and see how many you get. When I did, in 0.30 seconds I found 16,700 books, articles or web pages! Now I suspect many of the links are not actually real books. And I also imagine that many of these 16,700 search results only have a passing relationship to the topic of persuasion. I mean, what has Jane Austin's novel *Pride and Prejudice* got to do with persuasion? But there it was on page two! Her last novel was called *Persuasion* and was on page one of course, but in fairness, it is not really going to help improve your skills in this area.

Seriously though, there are many books on persuasion, and some are quite old. The ancient Greeks including Socrates and Aristotle were banging on about making rational decisions through the reasoned argument of known facts and opinions, otherwise known as persuasion, and that was 400 years BC. Through the ages, others have added to our understanding of the matter. For instance: Dale Carnegie who wrote *How to Win Friends and Influence People* in the 1930s; David Ogilvy who wrote the book with the punchiest title *Ogilvy on Advertising*; and Robert Cialdini who wrote *The Art and Science of Influence* in 1982.

So why did Nick and I set out to write another one on the same subject? Apart from needing the money…

Yes, we have a business to run, and yes, we have views on this subject (and quite a few other opinions too, to be fair) that we'd like others to read or hear about. It is also true that very few of the leading texts on persuasion have been written by everyday business people, like us, for ordinary business people, like you. Most are by academics or want-to-be-gurus aiming to name and command a new space like Neuromarketing or Buyology: The New Science of Desire.

Our aim is to set out a process that anyone can follow by explaining why each step is important and exactly how to use each level thoroughly. Our intention for this book is to improve your understanding of and skill at persuasion. Our ambition is that after reading this book and applying its principles, you will, more often and more readily, be able to secure 'willing support' from those around you.

Now you might be thinking, "Why didn't he say that about three pages ago?" Well, we are sales and marketing people at heart, so why use one word when two hundred will do?

By reading this book, you will understand the key steps to take yourself, as well as the steps that the other person or persons must go through, to get them from x to y; to communicate more efficiently. You will learn how to become more able to persuade others to modify their attitude and behaviour.

We hope and pray that your intentions are good, and your use of this approach to persuasion is based purely on your integrity for attaining genuinely positive outcomes for all involved, to lead a business, a family or a project more effectively, to communicate your ideas more persuasively in writing, one-to-one or when speaking to a group. And on that basis, we wish you well in applying these concepts, achieving your ambitions and creating a better result for everyone involved.

1
Context

In this section we will discover that while communication seems easy, it is harder to do effectively. To persuade we must communicate effectively. The need to persuade today is greater than ever before and is made more challenging because of the different modes of communication available as well as there often being a difference between what is communicated and what is received.

- We all have a need to persuade every day for one reason or another.
- What is said in my communication is not necessarily what is heard—why does it often go wrong?
- If I can improve my communication I improve my ability to persuade.
- Our life experiences shape how we see the world and how we receive communication, affecting how we might be persuaded.
- People experience change daily, and each person can respond to the same type of change differently to the way others might—understanding that will help us in our ability to persuade others.

Do we need the skill of persuasion?

Well, you'll only need the skill of persuasion if there are times in your life where others see things or want to do things differently from you. I'm sure it won't happen too often… at least not every day!

- Maybe your local council has changed collecting the rubbish from weekly to once a month to save money, and you don't think it is right?
- Maybe your teenagers have started smoking, and you think that is dumb?
- Maybe you have prospects who bring up objections which you struggle to answer?
- Maybe a person you are sweet on just won't go out with you?

Need I go on…?

The need for persuasion kicks in whenever you and one or more others end up in two separate places.

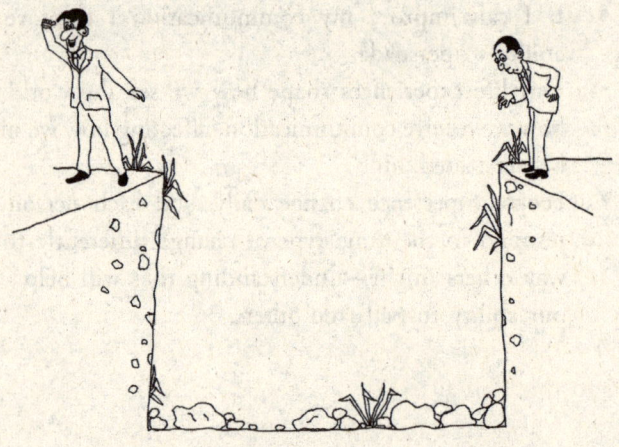

Picture two hills—with a valley in between—with one person on one side—one person on the other side—a steep, dangerous valley—an impossible gap—can't jump across—both people facing the same direction—one looking down—the other looking off into the distance.

You are entirely convinced it would be better for everyone involved if the other person(s) joined you on your side. The strategy or process of getting them across requires the skill of persuasion. You can't negotiate and meet them in the middle, and you cannot trade sides. Houston, we have a problem…

Well, at least two problems.

The first is that we've been through some thinking or maybe some 'life experiences' that led us to the point of drawing this conclusion, of taking up this position, of fixing this belief. We've been there, done it, got the T-shirt—you are on top of that hill, you own the hill and no one but no one is going to take that hill from you. We no longer have any form of confusion or any flicker of doubt and so have no active mental enquiry going on in our head. In fact, we think it is so normal and so obvious that our attention is elsewhere, we see a new horizon, a new issue or topic—that is our focus of attention and thought now. The bias is hardwired into our brain, and if anyone asks us about anything connected to the said hill, we'll trot out the default answer without even having to break sweat let alone engage the brain and think.

This means you may not understand or even appreciate the conclusion or position of those you wish to persuade because they may have been through a different set of experiences and therefore ended up in a different place. But, like you, they own a 'hill'—their hill—and don't usually trouble their conscious mind to think about it.

You will both have been through a thought process and

reflect or even experience feelings associated with pain or joy. The trouble is, you've forgotten the pain or the active thinking, you've already gone through the journey of confusion and doubt so what you now see as the truth, or as correct, you view through the rose-tinted glasses of someone who made it through the valley of fear. Strange as it may seem, it is hard to put yourself in the shoes of someone who doesn't see it like you. It is also hard to even think the way you did previously, before you arrived on your current hill. You may not be able to find a mental reference point of someone who has not started the journey to your hill. Most scary of all—some who haven't started the journey to your point of view will not even be able to see the mountain you are so confident of, because to them, in their world, your hill doesn't even exist.

The second problem is… whoever you are trying to persuade, even if they can see your hill, will recognise it as *their* hill, which is a different hill that will be separated from you by a deep and dark valley. If they must leave their point of view, they will only be able to see down. They may be intentionally looking the other way to avoid the darkness. They may have heard your initial call but are refusing to look your way.

But, if they are prepared to see things from your point of view, then this will steer them away from the initial danger of looking only down. You know the grass is greener on your side, you are familiar with the darkness, hard thinking, pain and confusion are temporary, you know it all works out right in the end because you've read the last page of the book. They haven't. No sir! To them, it just looks terrible. It looks like grief. Their journey must start with giving up their hill to begin a journey of discovery without any certainty of what the outcome will be for them. And nothing in this world is going to get any right-minded person to head in that downwards direction. Forgot it sugar—I am happy where I am. My hill is kinda green. I like it here. You cannot make me leave it.

Now if you prefer the academic answer to why we need the skill of persuasion, then look up 'The Change Curve'—there are plenty of them.

The commonly-quoted model was devised by Elizabeth Kubler Ross, a Swiss psychiatrist who worked extensively with the bereaved and dying and was a principal founder of the hospice movement. She noticed a pattern of reaction to news of impending death, which went through the stages of shock, denial, anger, bargaining, depression and finally acceptance. The theory, while untested in a traditional scientific way, gained immediate recognition and has since been applied widely to encompass almost any aspect of personal and corporate change.

Other alternatives include:

- 'The Personal Transition Curve' by John Fisher, as part of his work on Personal Construct Psychology. Rather than assessing the reaction to death, this is a study of changing behaviour. Here, the eight stages are listed as: Anxiety and Denial, Happiness, Fear, Threat, Guilt and Disillusionment, Depression and Hostility, Gradual Acceptance and Moving Forward.
- 'The Transtheoretical Model of Behaviour Change' by James O. Prochaska of the University of Rhode Island and his colleagues, describes a similar process with stages labelled Not Ready, Getting Ready, Ready, Action, Maintenance, and Termination or Zero temptation to return.
- The Lewis-Parker 'Transition Curve' with seven stages are summarised as follows: Immobilisation—Shock; Denial of Change—Temporary Retreat; Incompetence—

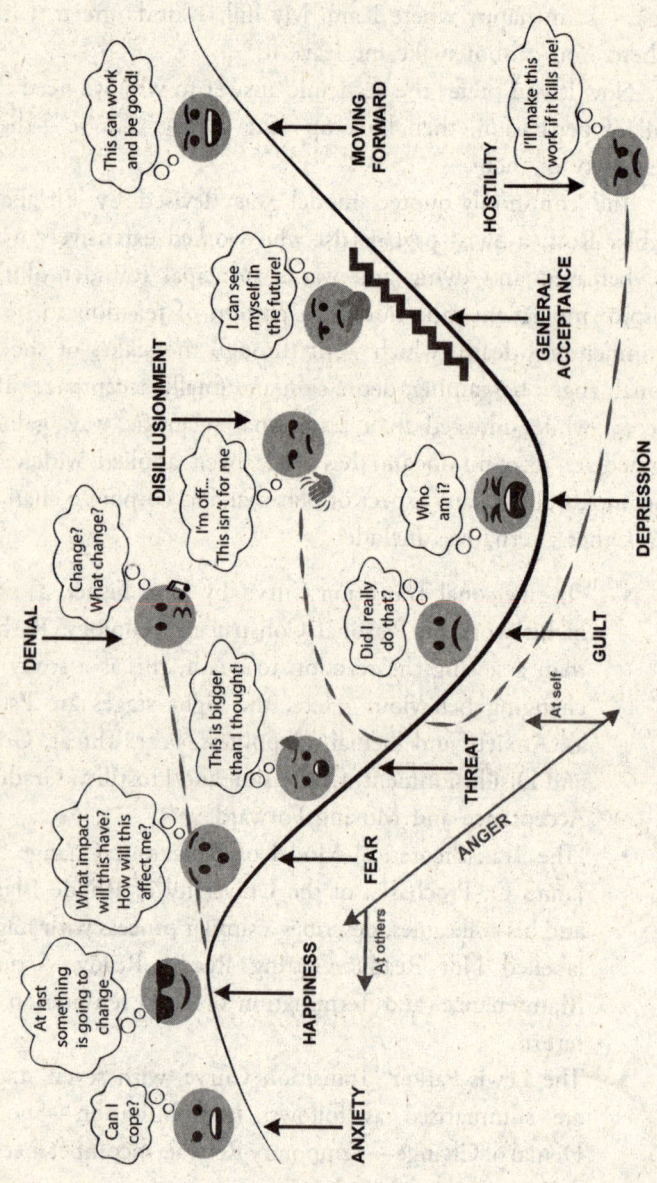

Awareness and Frustration; Acceptance of Reality—Letting Go; Testing—New ways to deal with new reality; Search for Meaning—Internalisation; Integration—Incorporation of meanings within behaviours.

Many people consider Nick and I, your authors, to be simple men, and in fairness, they are right. So, I offer you a simplified model that condenses the plethora of positions you could find yourself in on the change curve to four. Four stages of the U-bend of change. This represents a U-bend just like you'd see under your sink or behind your toilet bowl. And, on any self-respecting U-bend, there is no shortcut to avoid the curve; in our U-bend the only way to get from ignoring the need to change to acceptance of a new point of view is by going through the other two stages—argue and explore.

When people ignore the need to change it is as if they have fingers in their ears and blindfolds over their eyes, or as comedian Catherine Tate says so poetically, "Face bovvered? Not." People at this point in the change curve just don't see the point of even talking about it.

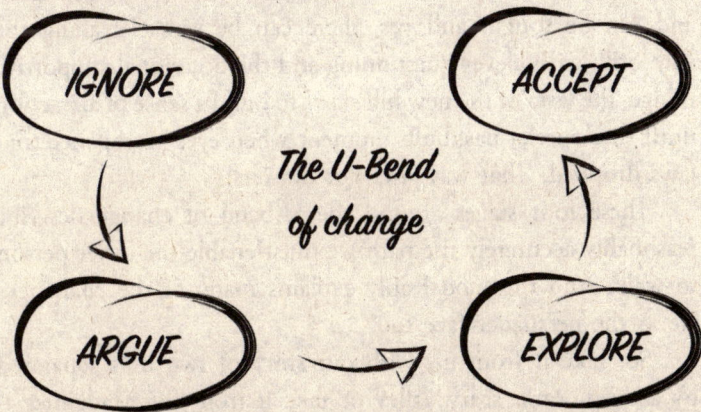

Stage two, or argue, is in fact progress. Hard to believe because now, instead of ignoring your ideas, they are fighting back and being generally critical of the concept or point of view you are proposing. Some may even be critical of you, let alone the hill you are standing on. One danger is that we sense this 'push-back' as a negative and argumentative stage in the journey and as a problem for us and the other person so backtrack or ease off a little. We hope for a more pleasant journey, so we reverse and head off in different directions in search of that elusive shortcut between ignoring and acceptance, only to find... it doesn't exist! In the meantime, our change of pace and direction has confused the other person even more.

In the end, if we persist, our colleague arrives at the explore stage where there is far more of a genuine interest in the ideas we've raised. Some are positive, some future based, some negative, and some backwards-looking at that wonderful deeply-held belief that they used to enjoy when sitting on their previous beautiful hill. Now they are genuinely engaging the power of thought, questioning and hypothesising, reflecting and discussing.

Once in the explore stage, the journey through the change curve takes on a different momentum and focus—yes, it is uphill and can be tough, and yes, there can be setbacks along the way. Still, with clever questioning and the occasional supportive nudge, the vista of the new hill starts to build a sense of attraction until that eureka flashbulb moment when eyes are opened and jaws dropped. That was jaws not drawers!

These four stages around the U-bend of change describe reasonably accurately the path we must enable the other person to walk. And the model ably explains many of the challenges we as the persuader face too.

So, take it from us, with our story of two hills separated by a deep, dark, scary valley or take it from the academics—

you thought this persuasion thing was easy… Just smile nicely, sensibly, and clearly explain things, and hey-presto, job done! Well maybe—sometimes. Then again, more often you are likely to have to deal with some reluctance or some resistance to your charm offensive and a mixture of facts, arguments and emotion.

QED = you need this skill of persuasion…

How we see the world

How did we come to our point of view? And why is it so hard at times to see or believe another view? We all interact with the world from a unique perspective—our own! This interaction includes all our past experiences, and because of what we make of those experiences, means our view of the world often dictates how we approach situations, what we believe, who we believe, as well as what and who we don't.

As we live and grow, succeed and fail, we are continually observing, assimilating, developing actions/reactions, experimenting and testing beliefs. If we have a degree of self-awareness, then we are, even non-consciously, conducting on-going research and development, examining ourselves and our ideas along with our views on the world.

How we interact with other people is also the result of our past experiences and an assessment of the current situation which is then mapped onto possible alternative courses of action. We generate a hypothesis about what will happen if we do or say x instead of y, and then chose that course of action which we think will best suit our needs. This may or may not take any other people involved into account.

We are not victims of circumstance; we do have the power to change our views, our attitudes and our behaviour. And yet, we are limited strongly in some ways. The opinion defines us as a person, our abilities and potential. We are limited by our view on our current position and the relationships we have. We are limited by our own internal blinkers. These limit how far out into the future we dare look, as well as the range of possible options we can see for ourselves, and hence restrict our ability to accept things outside the frames of reference we currently hold.

Our collection of experiences and actions form our mental picture of the world and each idea, each thing or each person we consider we will place on our map, somewhere between two fixed points. Those points are the extreme ends of our views on the matter. Based on our perceptions of other people and what they say or do, we place them somewhere between those two markers as part of our map of the world. We also place ourselves somewhere in relation to the position we've allocated to them, either near to us or far away. We use that map and our relative position to others, to things and to beliefs as a guide. This guide helps us to choose not only our behaviours but also our friends and our beliefs.

As part of life, we are constantly taking part in live R&D. We are continually assessing things for their level of 'fit' within our world. With low levels of awareness, sometimes called default thinking, fast thinking or thin slicing, we don't even notice that we've opted in or out of a situation. With high levels of self-awareness, we would be testing the validity of our map and the places we allocate to people and things. That slow thinking takes time, effort and energy, and probably none of us could cope with a constant reassessment of our mental maps. There is just not enough energy to get through the day if we tried. Of course, a short burst of high intensity is possible, and so every now and then we tend to get serious about our thinking thus enabling us to redraw those maps. Sadly, not everyone will willingly put in the thought, time, effort and energy. Some people won't or can't, at least not voluntarily, redraw their map.

The building blocks of our map come in various shapes and sizes. Some aspects are more important and are connected to our 'core' or sense of being. These are very resistant to change and include things such as right versus wrong, our moral code and religious beliefs. A threat or challenge to our core is normally met with significant resistance. Other building blocks are more peripheral. A suggestion that invites us to change them does not have the same impact. The rest fall somewhere in between and unconsciously are ranked against or connected to the others. Some building blocks we think of in an all-or-nothing way, like a ball is a ball and cannot be anything else. Some come with a whole batch of ancillary stereotyped baggage attached to them. Whether this is right or wrong doesn't matter—if we think real men don't cry so be it. Thankfully some of our building blocks are quite movable, a bit like a Rubik's Cube: providing the blue face is on the blue side, then everything is fine.

To be able to communicate with another person, let alone persuade them, we need to have some understanding of how the other person perceives their world and where we and our 'Big Idea' fit into it. By having a knowledge of this we will determine their reaction to our world, or whether we are able to work out some aspects of their map ahead of time, enabling us to find more efficient points of reference, make it more relevant and be able to persuade them more easily.

For example, Bob and his wife Julie were on holiday in a quiet village in Fuerteventura. Bob described the story like this:

> *"The original plan was to get a villa near a village with its own pool and do nothing for the week—just chill. Part way through the week, while strolling back from the village after a*

late wine-fuelled lunch, we stopped to look into the window of a tourist attraction shop. While easily disregarding most of the attractions, the hire of a three-wheel motorbike did catch my eye. With the warm weather, and tiny winding roads that snake around the small island of Fuerteventura, the idea of touring on one of those powerful bikes appealed to me.

So, I suggested it... only to be met with firm and abrupt resistance. Back and forth went the conversation. OK, the argument. This argument went on for five or so minutes until my brain kicked back in. My wife's elder brother had died in a motorbike accident when she was seven years old, and while she happily gets on a pedal bike, she has only ever been on a motorbike twice in her life and hated every second. I might suggest a three-wheeler is safer and that the roads are less dangerous until I was blue in the face.

On this topic with a belief central to the core of her being the three-wheeler tour discussion was going nowhere. The attraction of the three-wheeler ride was not important enough for me and certainly not important enough for Julie to even consider. That 'Big Idea' was never going to fit into her world where motorbikes are closely connected to such a massive and painful loss. I'd like to think that had it not been for the wine then I would never have suggested it, but that is probably not true because I've been fascinated with motorbikes since I was a four-year-old."

That personal example highlights the importance of understanding the core beliefs of the parties involved. The emotional attraction to, or rejection of, the Big Idea may have little to do with the current situation, and may have more to do with unconnected things from light years away in another lifetime.

Theories of communication

In some ways, of course, our ability to persuade is directly linked to our ability to communicate. The personal situation above could be used to explain one of the leading theories on how communication works or doesn't. That model is owed to Wilbur Schramm, a well-known communication theorist, who developed a straightforward communication model in his book *The Process and Effects of Mass Communications*.

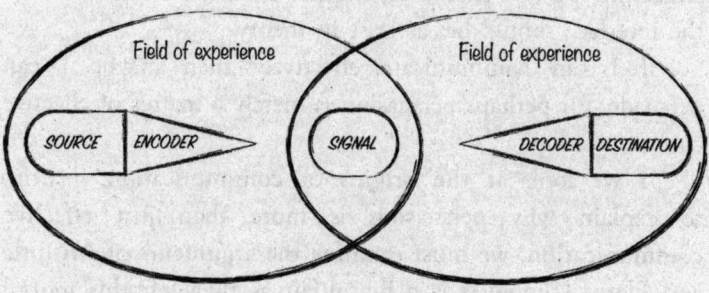

Schramm's first model suggests, as did Aristotle, that communication always contains three main elements—the source, the message and the destination. In the simple version, the source encodes a signal and then transmits it to the target destination via a selected channel, where it is received and hopefully decoded to create the same meaning that it had contained before being encoded by the source.

Schramm also pointed out that for the intent and content of the message to be encoded and decoded so that a calibration of understanding or a common understanding can take place between the source and the destination, the 'Source' and 'Destination' must share something in common.

That means the fields of experience of the source and the destination must overlap in some way before effective communication can take place. If your mental map of the world is entirely separate from mine and we have no shared experiences whatsoever, then even at the most basic level of communication we are not going to understand and relate to one another. Such shared experiences could include language and culture as well as the physical environment. Where we share a small area of overlap, then communication is not impossible, just tricky. The larger the space of shared experiences the more straightforward the interface should be, at least in theory.

If I can communicate effectively then maybe I can persuade. Or perhaps persuasion is merely a matter of effective communication?

If we look at the origins of communication theories to explain why persuasion is more than just effective communication, we must examine the arguments of Aristotle and Plato. I know it is a bit unfair as they left this mortal coil some time ago, but this is what happens when you've been famous for so long!

Aristotle's Model of Communication

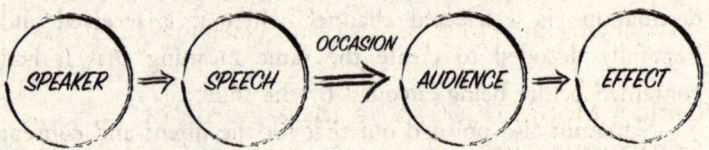

Aristotle's main point was that to create the desired effect as a speaker you need to have an accurate insight or understanding of your audience and the situation. Armed with those ideas, you would then be able to prepare a different speech depending on the audience and the occasion. Conversely, if you thought you could deliver the same talk to a different audience at another time and still create precisely the same effect, you would need to be seen by a psychiatrist!

Lasswell's Model

Harold Lasswell, a political scientist, developed a much-quoted formulation of the main elements of communication: "Who says what in which channel to whom with what effect."

This summation of the communication process has been widely quoted since the 1940s. The point in Lasswell's view is that there must be an 'effect' for communication to take place. An 'effect' is described as an observable or measurable change in the audience or listener; meaning that if we have communicated effectively, the receiver changes in some way.

Lasswell's version of the communication process mentions four parts—who, what, channel, whom. Aristotle also talks about three of the four parallel sections—speaker (who), subject (what), the person addressed (whom). Only 'channel' was added by Lasswell after over 1000 years. A smart fellow, that Mr A.

Berlo's Model (1960): The Ingredients of Communication

Berlo's model shows many of the critical elements used in the communication process. These factors contain variable characteristics of the sender and the receiver and affect their communication ability and the quality of understanding achieved. This model is sometimes known as the SMCR Model (Source, Message, Channel, Receiver).

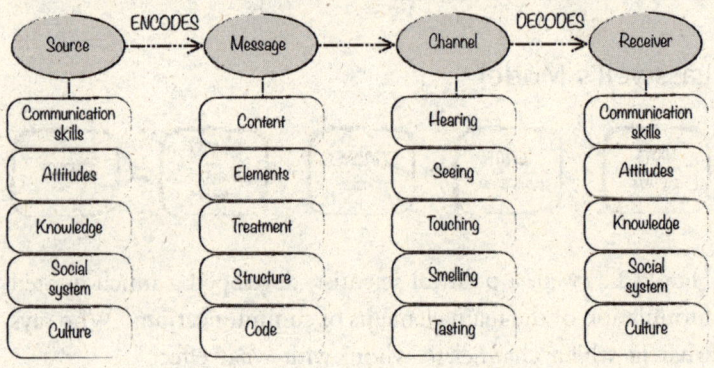

Each of these theories falls within the realm of understanding the process of communication.

Semiotics

Another route we can travel down to understand communication is titled 'The Semiotics School', the foundations of which were laid by Charles Morris in the 1930s through the study of signs and symbols. This school of thinking approaches communication as the generation of meaning via a mixture of signs, symbols and messages. The sender selects a set of signs and symbols to convey a specific purpose of creating a particular reaction from the receiver.

Some proponents of the process school of communication call semantics 'the noise' which can interfere with communication. We each assign meaning to words, to voice inflexions in speech, to gestures and expressions and to other similar 'noises' in writing. We don't all assign the same meaning to the same sign, symbol or word and so end up with a severe problem or barrier to effective communication, a barrier many do not realise until too late, if at all. Too often the person sending a message chooses to use words, phrases or symbols that have a specific meaning to him or her. However, those same words, phrases and symbols may have a significantly different meaning to individuals receiving the message. The encoding and decoding of the embedded meanings are massively crucial for effective communication to take place, and unless we are communicating effectively and in harmony, we will probably never persuade anyone of anything.

The different outcomes

We've looked at the process of communication and the semantic school of thought and yet we've barely mentioned the impact of any of this communication theory on the receiver.

William McGuire (1981) adds a further dimension to communication. Instead of having only 'input factors' with Source, Message, Channel and Receiver, he added 'output' factors of Attention, Liking, Comprehension, Yielding, Remembering and Action. McGuire's focus was the 'effect' the communication has on the receiver. Everyone from Aristotle on mentioned this and yet few studied it as profoundly as McGuire.

For many purposes of communication, his model of outputs can be displayed like this

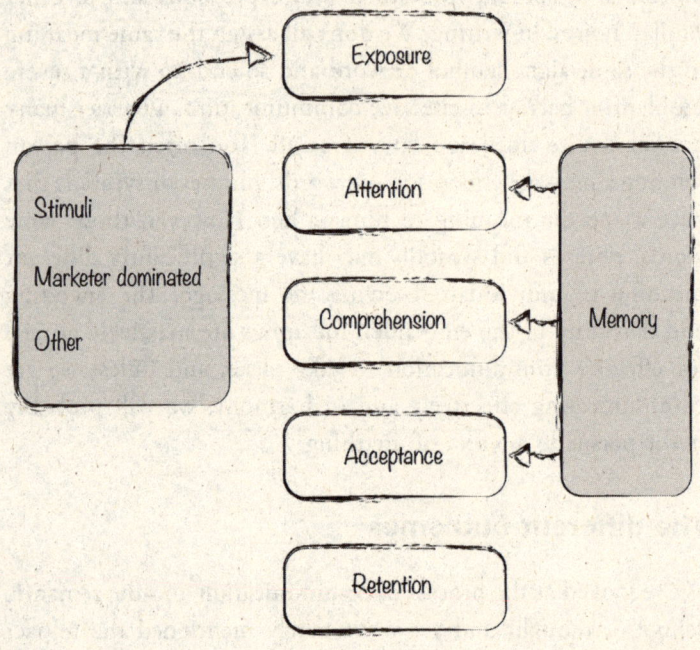

Someone has heard, liked, understood and accepted our message. That message is now successfully planted in the receiver's brain. This works when you are trying to inform, educate or teach someone French or Mathematics. It just isn't the full monty when you need to persuade someone. Thankfully, McGuire did a great job, and so, when considering persuasion as the purpose of communication, we can reflect on the full model which he even called a model of persuasion.

Not all communication is about persuasion although many consider it to be the toughest part of the job. This means that to have a hope of persuading others to your point-of-view, you will need to have a pretty good understanding of the essential skills of communication. You must understand the three aspects

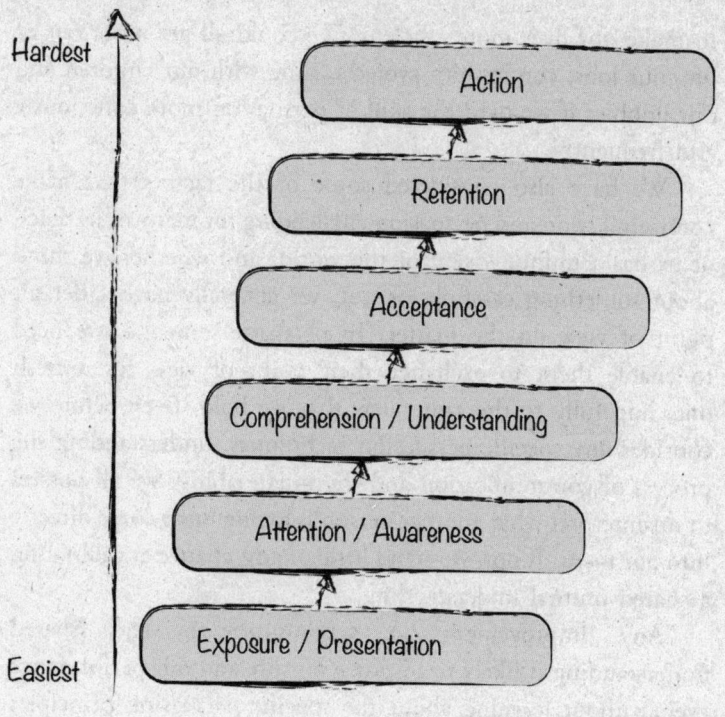

of communication we've discussed: process, the semantics and the outcomes. If you have a grasp of these elements, you will be sufficiently self-aware to understand your mental model of the world; but you must also be wise and appreciate that you need to understand the other person's mental map as well as you can. If you cannot understand another's map, you must be willing to work further on your crucial communication skills.

SUMMARY

In this chapter we have considered why persuasion is an everyday skill for most people and how it can make a positive contribution to make our lives more efficient. We could all get more out of life, our jobs, community projects, time with our children and our hobbies if we used the skill of persuasion more consciously and frequently.

We have also considered some of the factors that make communication and persuasion challenging for many of us. Each of us has a unique vision of the world, and whether we think about something carefully or not, we generally have a default point of view on the matter. To persuade someone, we need to enable them to exchange their point of view for a fresh one, hopefully to the same view that we hold. Even before we consider any specific persuasion techniques, understanding the process of communication and the innate ability we all possess to misinterpret what another person is saying must come directly into our focus. If not, we stand little, if any, chance at calibrating a shared mutual understanding.

Any improvement in communication and shared understanding is likely to improve our life and our performance even without learning about the specific persuasion principles and concepts in the following chapters.

Of course, we hope you continue to read the chapter on the PERSUADE model because it will provide you with a practical tool to help you plan and apply an efficient approach to persuasion. In the meantime, you have already gained some significant ideas, so it is appropriate to offer you some time to reflect and absorb your learning.

REFLECT AND LEARN

What ideas from this chapter were novel, fresh or new to you? What have you learned that was familiar? In what ways do you already apply some of this information?

How did you react emotionally and cognitively to the ideas in this chapter? What concepts do you agree with and why? What do you disagree with and why?

What were the most exciting or useful insights gained from reading and thinking about this chapter?

In what ways might you translate the ideas presented through this chapter into practical, everyday, useful ideas and plans?

What new questions about persuasion do you now have after reading this chapter?

ACTION LEARNING

In addition to the original three examples you selected at the beginning of the book, list several other people and situations where you could apply your learning of persuasion.

Set yourself some time-phased goals to apply some of the learning that you listed in the Reflect and Learn section, to guide your actions over the next three months, some for the next three weeks and some for the next three days.

Thinking about how you plan to apply your learning, what obstacles might you encounter along the way? And, realistically, how might you deal with them?

Who else could you share these ideas with as a supportive sounding board, or as your informal coach? How might you go about setting up a conversation with them to enrol them as a supporter of the application of your learning? Consider what might be the reasons why they would consider being involved? How might they also benefit?

2
The Basis of Persuasion

The basis of persuasion

Why is it that some people seem better able to persuade than others? Why is it that some communication is persuasive and some not? Having the right elements in your communication optimises your ability to persuade. This section considers these points and what we can do about them.

- The more you connect with the person, the better your chances of persuading.
- Why trust and credibility are so important when persuading and what we can do about it.
- Asking questions is key to successful persuasion.

- If the other person feels I care and understand their needs, I will considerably increase my chances of successful persuasion.
- Relying solely on logical reasons to persuade is a recipe for failure. Why?

Ethos, Pathos, Logos

The challenge of being able to influence and persuade has been a part of our existence for some considerable time. The ability to bring about a change or shift in the way someone thinks or behaves, to get someone to act or do something differently, is as topical today as it was thousands of years ago.

A lot of what we know and do today is arguably based on the philosophies and teachings of some of the great Greek philosophers from over 3,000 years ago. The most commonly accepted and used principles of persuasion today are based on Ethos, Pathos & Logos, and on the teachings of such great Greek philosophers such as Plato, Socrates and Aristotle.

- Ethos—Personal credibility
- Pathos—Empathy
- Logos—Logical argument

These three are sequential, so it is essential that each one is established in turn within the relationship that persuasion is occurring. Establishing credibility first is critical as without it the other person is unlikely to listen, pay attention or believe what the other person is saying.

Having established personal credibility, then the persuader (the person seeking to persuade the other) will attempt to understand the other person and see things from their point of view. If this appeals to the other person and common ground might be established, then the person being persuaded is more likely to listen to the persuader when it comes to putting across their point of view.

Finally, you will need to make a logical argument that makes sense to the person you'd like to persuade. The only way to reach this stage is for the persuader to understand the points that are important to the person being influenced, by positioning your 'proposal' or 'point of view' in such a way that it makes sense to them. They, of course, are more likely to listen to the proposal because they feel that the persuader is credible (Ethos), clearly understands their point of view and their challenges (Pathos) and are therefore inclined to see the value (Logos) in what is being suggested (your idea).

So, let's consider how important these three points are when it comes to successful persuasion.

Ethos—personal credibility

We tend to believe people whom we respect. Our goal when seeking to persuade someone is to project an impression on the other person that you are credible and worth listening to, as well as being likeable and worthy of respect. It's like having your own brand image.

The strength of a brand image is reflected in the extent to which it attracts potential customers. It is, in general, the first thing a potential customer will associate with a product.

Well, just as products have a brand image, so do we. Everyone has a brand image. Your brand image is representative of what other people perceive you stand for. It is often regarded as the first 'hurdle' in our attempt to be heard and believed.

Years ago, a particular make of car from an Eastern Bloc country was considered highly unreliable and became the butt of all car jokes. As a result, few people were really interested in owning one. Even though the car may have had a good story to tell and the challenges and frustrations of its customers were understandable, few potential buyers wanted to hear about this because they were unable to overcome the first hurdle: the hurdle of credibility. Interestingly, all of that has changed today with the advancement of technology, and the same cars are now considered highly superior in virtually all areas.

So we, as individuals, have a brand image also, one that represents the first hurdle we must all overcome. We want our prospects to accept and believe we are personally credible as this will determine how successful we are.

So, what helps give me credibility?

Several things lend themselves to establishing credibility in another's eyes, although each one, of course, will not have the same effect and gravitas with everyone. One factor may mean a considerable amount to one person, whereas it may say absolutely nothing to someone else.

- **Your qualifications**—academic, vocational
- **Track record**—how you are perceived through your past achievements
- **Skills**—specialist or any other skills you perform effectively
- **Knowledge**—understanding that when applied demonstrates wisdom
- **Reputation**—a widespread opinion about you
- **Position**—whether you hold a senior job as well as fitting into a niche
- **People you associate with**—your network of people. Who you associate with speaks volumes about you

No doubt there may be other factors, but those above are the primary considerations. Any of these might be sufficient to get you to a point where you can establish initial credibility—although it may not be enough to keep your credibility intact.

> **Activity—think of someone who you would like to influence. Now consider what will give you initial credibility in their eyes.**
>
> What will give me personal credibility in their eyes?
>
> -
> -
> -
> -
>
> Which one of these do I consider will have the strongest influence on them?
>
> How could I do this?

What contributes to keeping my credibility intact?

Credibility is a fragile and delicate creature and keeping it intact is based on how you act in each situation. Your credibility needs looking after and, if it is fragile, can break very easily.

As an example, one cannot help thinking about Gerald Ratner and the rather unfortunate turn of events during a speech he gave to the Institute of Directors on 23 April 1991. During the speech, he commented:

"We also offer cut-glass sherry decanters complete with six glasses on a silver-plated tray that your butler can serve you drinks on, all for £4.95. People say, 'How can you sell this for such a low price?' I say, 'Because it's total crap.'"

He was stupid enough to compound this by going on to remark that some of the earrings were ..."Cheaper than an M&S prawn sandwich but probably wouldn't last as long".

After the speech, the value of the Ratner group plummeted by around £500 million, which, not surprisingly, almost resulted in the firm's collapse. Ratner resigned in November 1992, and the company changed its name to Signet Group in September 1993.

You could argue very strongly that before he made that speech on that day in that room his credibility with his audience had been healthy, based on his previous track-record, reputation and position. But, almost in an instant, by criticising his products, his entire credibility went flying out of the window. He had been a fool to himself, and although he may have intended his comments as a joke, the reputation of his company was lost, along with his own.

So, the truth is that people judge us by our actions, not our intentions. However, we tend to judge ourselves by our intentions rather than our actions. To understand how to keep credibility, you must consider the individual you wish to persuade. Why? Because each person uniquely defines credibility. What one person determines you need to do to remain credible, may well be very different from the definition the next person places on your reliability and reputation. Furthermore, you must be careful, because the way one person perceives your credibility may also define how others associated with that person may see you.

However, consider the following scenarios as an example of the way different people may have entirely opposing expectations of you.

- **Telephone conference call**—What someone may have required you to do before the call, during the call and after the call may differ from one person to the next. Consider what types of behaviour they like or appreciate. What might really irritate or annoy them in such a setting?
- **Face-to-face meeting**—How does the other person view building rapport? Consider what subjects you might avoid. Are there subjects close to their heart? I remember having a senior internal colleague at the *Daily Mail* who always required me to prepare well in advance for such a meeting and would judge me on whether I turned up either late and without preparation. For me to be considered credible in his eyes, I needed to be on time, be well equipped, get down to business rapidly and be prepared to have an opinion about the subject at hand. I was also expected to be prepared to challenge the 'norm' rather than nod in sycophantic agreement.
- **Questioning**—The quality of your questioning can have a direct bearing on the amount of credibility you are perceived to possess. The better and more thoughtful the question, the more reliability you are likely to have. If you can inject a well-considered form of questioning that takes everyone's thought process in a different direction by considering something from another perspective, then you are likely to be found more credible by your actions in each situation.

- **Being in front of others**—You may have all the right qualifications, knowledge and even the highest position, but unless that is backed up with applied experience, it won't count for much. How you choose to use your knowledge in a situation can be interpreted as wisdom. One can never forget the old adage: 'It is better to close your mouth and be thought a fool—than to open it and remove all doubt.'
- **Giving/receiving feedback**—Not everyone loves to either give or receive feedback, or both. Although feedback is meant to be regarded as a gift, it is important to remember that most gifts are carefully wrapped, and consideration is given to when and how this reward is presented. It's the same with feedback. Unless you think carefully about how you present feedback (remember, you will always need to consider the other person to do this), then your credibility can be irretrievably damaged. A wrong word here, a wrong word there, will carry more weight than all the positive feedback you may give. Remember, if you utter a 'wrong' word, people will linger on it.

  It is the same with positive feedback. Mark Twain said: "Man can live off a compliment for two weeks." Are you good at **receiving** feedback? You can enhance your credibility by asking for feedback, welcoming feedback and being seen to act on it. Conversely, if you are defensive, and do not pursue feedback, this might cause an adverse reaction to your credibility.

What's the point of all this?

The point, of course, is always to consider the individual whom you wish to persuade. These are all examples, but bear in mind that credibility is based on what we do—and not on what we intend to do. Remember, you must consider both the person and the situation you are likely to find yourself in to establish or protect your credibility.

> **Activity—what behaviours could act to reinforce and enhance your credibility?**
>
> 1. Think of the person
>
> 2. Think of the situation
>
> 3. Think of what you need to do with that person in that situation to keep your credibility intact, if not build it.

Pathos—empathy

Some years ago on an American television news channel, a reporter was interviewing a man in the street. He was being asked about what the (then) President Bush had said on TV the previous evening about the economy. The reporter asked him if he was at all influenced by what the President had suggested that the American people should do about the situation that the President discussed.

The man's reply was impressive. "I am not at all influenced by what the President said and won't listen to him." He continued: "After all, he never listens to us!" The message was loud and clear. To have any chance of influencing someone you must first be sure to communicate that you understand the challenges the audience faces and that you care. In other words, you must demonstrate by proving that you care.

- What is empathy?
- Seeing it from the other person's point of view.
- Understanding their thoughts, hopes, fears and what they want?

The key here is to demonstrate empathy. You may ask why this is important; well, consider this...

You can act upon all the above in your mind without demonstrating it. However, what might the perception be that you create by doing so? It will suggest that you don't care. If the other person **feels** you don't care, then why should they listen to you and your ideas? So, it becomes the 'action' rather than the intent of what you do. This step must either be to demonstrate that you understand, or at least have the desire and make an effort to understand the other person's point of view. Remember, people judge you by your actions—not by your intentions.

How do I demonstrate empathy?

Socrates suggested that empathy is the 'pursuit of understanding'. It is exposing to the other person that your real intention is to understand them.

Once you can demonstrate you have empathy for the other person, you can then appeal to their emotions and build a strong bond of connection. Consider the following example from Martin Luther King:

> *"I am not unmindful that some of you have come here out of great trials and tribulations. Some of you have come fresh from narrow jail cells. And some of you have come from areas where your quest—the quest for freedom left you battered by the storms of persecution and staggered by the winds of police brutality. You have been the veterans of creative suffering. Continue to*

work with the faith that unearned suffering is redemptive. Go back to Mississippi, go back to Alabama, go back to South Carolina, go back to Georgia, go back to Louisiana, go back to the slums and ghettos of our northern cities, knowing that somehow this situation can and will be changed."

I Have a Dream by Martin Luther King Jr. 28th August 1963.

Clearly, this is a great example of Martin Luther King connecting with the pain and emotions of his audience by saying:

- "I understand."
- "I know where you are coming from."
- "I fully appreciate how you might be feeling."

All of these are critical to establishing empathy. How else can you demonstrate compassion on a very day-to-day practical level with someone? You can do this in any number of ways although some of the more obvious might be through …

Questions

If you ask the right questions, not only are you demonstrating that you are pursuing an understanding which, in turn, will enhance your perceived empathy, but might it also affect something else? Might it impact on your credibility? Of course, it would! The fact you are asking questions combined with the quality and depth of the information you are seeking says a lot about you, your thought processes and your real intentions.

We will cover more about questioning as we move into the PERSUADE model later in the book, but suffice to say that such questioning is an integral, fundamental and the most powerful tool used in the influencing process.

Listening

What good is cheese without crackers? What is the benefit of bread without butter? What good is questioning if you are not prepared to listen? The answer is—not much! As Frank Sinatra once sang, they go together like 'a horse and carriage'.

It is therefore worth considering the difference between **passive** listening and **active** listening. 'Passive' listening is, as the title denotes—passive. In other words, you need do very little but merely listen. Your role is not intended to be that active. But, what sort of a message might this send to the person you are listening to? The fact you are not really listening? That you don't care? That may not be true, but if that is the perception being created, then that is the truth. Remember, people judge you by your actions—not your intentions.

'Active' listening is when your role as a listener is active! This means you must do things to demonstrate that you are listening. There are certain ways you can show that you are actively involved in the listening process, including:

Note taking—taking notes aids the listening process, allows you to summarise and clarify understanding, along with demonstrating to the other person that they are being heard and that you are 'pursuing' that understanding.

I'm-listening noises—a more fundamental yet human form of connection that continues to send out signals to the other person to assure them that you are receiving and understanding their message, and you encourage them to keep talking.

Visual body language clues—it is argued that the largest proportion of our communication is through visible contributions. The body gives off visual signs that demonstrate that you are either listening with empathy or not. Such hints could be eye contact, smiling, nodding, hand gestures and even sitting upright or leaning toward the other person.

Summarising—*It is better to be understood a little than to be misunderstood a lot* (Anatole France). A common myth about summarising is that it is performed by one person (although anyone involved can do it) and that the best time to summarise a situation is at the end, when, in reality, it should be done as you go.

Asking questions about what has been said—questions could be used to explore further what has been reported to seek an understanding or to build on what the speaker has said. Providing the subject of your question is linked explicitly to the theme of what the speaker has told you, then they will consider you have been listening and are taking an active interest in their ideas—always a good move when it comes to empathy!

Making statements

Making statements (not unlike Martin Luther King) that undoubtedly appeal to the emotion of the person you are trying to persuade, and that connect with any issues close to their heart and to matters that concern them, to demonstrate that you see, understand, and feel what they have said.

All these factors should be taken into consideration when it comes to Empathy. Empathy is all about focusing on the other person through the conversation, the questions you ask, your understanding and through the body language you express. The more a person feels cared about, that their point of view matters and their needs are understood and considered necessary, the more they are likely to be ready to receive a message that falls in line with what they have said. Indeed, they would welcome such a message!

> **Activity—How could you build and develop Empathy with someone?**
>
> 1. Think of the person.
>
> 2. Think of the situation.
>
> 3. What questions could you ask?
>
> What statement could you make to that person that clearly demonstrates you understand their point of view in relation to the subject being discussed?

That leads us on to the third part of this sequential influencing model—Logos.

Logos—logical argument and reasoning

Aristotle was known as the father of the field of logic. He was the first to develop a formalised system for reasoning. Aristotle observed that the validity of any argument can be determined by its structure rather than its content. As the person who wishes to persuade, we seek to appeal to the other person by connecting to their sense of logic and reasoning, in a way that makes perfect sense to them.

Logos is logical appeal, and the term logic is derived from it. It is normally used to describe facts and figures that support the speaker's topic. Since data is difficult to manipulate, especially if from a trusted source, logos may sway cynical listeners. Having a logos appeal can also enhance ethos (see above) because information makes the speaker look more knowledgeable and better prepared for his or her audience. Watch out though, data can be confusing and thus confuse the audience. Logos can also be misleading or inaccurate.

Interestingly, many people in their haste rely on this one element to get their point across to persuade. In doing so, they neglect the other two principles, those of credibility and empathy. They may feel that by putting across the facts and reason alone will be sufficient for the other person to act. Think about this for a second. Have you ever received an advertising proposition (through the post maybe?) that makes perfect sense for you to act on the message, but then you don't follow up? How about the opportunity to change your utility provider and save £250 a year in the process? Have you ever received anything along these lines and done anything about changing supplier?

Logically everyone should act by changing provider to save money, but the majority of people do not—somewhat proving the point that we do not makes decisions solely based on logical reasons.

An example of Logos

"Let us begin with a simple proposition: What democracy requires is public debate, not information. Of course, it needs information too, but the kind of information it needs can be generated only by vigorous popular debate. We do not know what we need to know until we ask the right questions, and we can identify the right questions only by subjecting our ideas about the world to the test of public controversy. Information, usually seen as the precondition of debate, is better understood as its by product. When we get into arguments that focus and fully engage our attention, we become avid seekers of relevant information. Otherwise, we take in information passively—if we take it in at all."

Christopher Lasch, *The Lost Art of Political Argument*

This Logos appeal involves convincing your audience that you are intelligent and the information you are providing can be trusted. We cannot simply say to our audience, "I can be trusted because I'm a very clever person". You have to prove yourself by demonstrating that you understand what you are talking about because:

- you are providing personal experience, or
- you have deep insights from someone else who has personal experience, or
- you are using generally accepted authorities on this topic
- through extensive and up-to-date research.

You appeal to the logical thought processes in your audience when you offer credible evidence to support your argument. That evidence includes:

- Facts—Non-debatable data widely accepted as the truth
- Examples—Including situations and topics that your audience can relate to
- Precedent—Specific examples from the past
- Authority—Someone, or an organisation, generally accepted as qualified to judge the topic in a relevant way at the time
- Logical reasoning—This will take one or more forms: Deductive, Inductive or Abductive reasoning

A short explanation of logical reasoning

Deductive Reasoning—when you slice and dice evidence to reach conclusions.

In general terms, deductive reasoning is using a given set of facts or data to deduce other facts from by following a step-by-step process. Deductive reasoning can be used to prove that these new facts are true. Here is a classic example:

- Major premise: All humans are mortal
- Minor premise: Socrates is human
- Conclusion: Socrates is mortal

Deductive reasoning provides no new information, it simply rearranges information that is already known into new statements or truths.

Inductive Reasoning—when you go beyond the evidence to reach new conclusions.

This is about looking for a pattern or a trend and then extrapolating from it or generalising from it. This tends to mean that you don't know for sure if this trend or conclusion will be 100% true.

An example is that all swans are white. We could draw that

conclusion from hours of walking around various lakes, as every swan we saw was white, none of them were black, so we could logically assume that black swans don't exist. While inductive reasoning can be helpful in exploring trends and establishing new conclusions, it can be risky.

Abductive Reasoning—when you add things together to draw new conclusions.

You could say that this is a form of guessing, since conclusions are drawn based on probabilities. The authentic aim is to find the most plausible conclusion, which hopefully is also the correct one. Example:

- Major premise: The jar is filled with chocolate buttons
- Minor premise: Nick has some chocolate buttons in his hand
- Conclusion: The chocolate buttons in Nick's hand were taken out of the jar

By abductive reasoning, it is possible that Nick took a handful of chocolate buttons from the jar. It is also pure speculation. The buttons in Nick's hand may never have been in the jar, they could have been bought at a shop separately, or someone may have given Nick the buttons. While we would authentically aim to draw the correct conclusion, abductive reasoning can lead to a false conclusion.

Use an appropriate writing or speaking style

When laying out the logical parts of your proposition, by all means use relevant, professional and strong words that carry the appropriate connotations; just be sure that you don't sound overly emotional. Sometimes that can be helped by using mostly the 3rd person and only using the 1st person when stating a specific personal experience. At times, it could be as simple as saying, "A generally accepted view is" rather than "My view is".

Refuting another's fact or opinion

This requires at least a health warning, if not a separate chapter. If you have to refute statements of fact, or more likely the conclusions drawn by others from different facts—you must at least demonstrate that you are treating your audience with respect by establishing some common ground first.

Find some mutual ground for both sides of the argument by acknowledging that your opinion and the opinion of the opposite side agree on at least one aspect. Show you are able to treat the topic fairly and your credibility will rise.

Be careful of the words you use

While we can all look up the dictionary definition of a word, no one is going to do so when in the middle of a conversation. Words, whether written or spoken, often carry secondary meanings, undertones and implications. For example, if you were to ask a friend who cares about their image how he or she would like to be described from the following list of words, what do you think the answer would be?

Slender................................Thin....................................Scrawny

While all the words carry the same denotation or dictionary definition (they all mean lean, and not fat), the word slender carries more positive undertones suggesting gracefulness and elegance. Scrawny suggests being overly thin and even unhealthy, whereas thin on the other hand is a fairly neutral word. Conclusion? Slender is the most likely answer because it contains more positive connotations.

The best way to avoid wrecking a logical proposition, as well as pathos (or emotional) appeal, is by using words that carry appropriate connotations.

Think about this statement: "I am not a crack addict. I am not a welfare benefit scrounger. I am not illiterate."

Compare it to this: "I am not a person who abuses substances. I have a job and do not receive welfare benefits. I can read."

The words crack addict, welfare scrounger and illiterate carry strong connotations. It makes the above statement, while already logical, more emotional. In some situations, it might be appropriate to use the stronger language, with more emotional appeal—in others the emotion will detract from your logic. Finding the best balance of logic and emotion is the ideal.

There are even some fairly neutral words that carry more persuasive weight. For instance:

Persuasive words	**Weak words**
Because	Can't
Definite	Problem
Success	Difficulty
Results	
Opportunities	**Wishy-washy words**
Gain	Maybe
Save	Possibly
Improve	Could
Reduce	Not sure
How it will help you is…	
The way you'll benefit is…	
The reasons why this is a good idea is…	

So, what's the point of these three Greek amigos?

The key message about this sequential model is to consider each element whenever you are aiming to persuade someone. Consider the extent to which you can become established with that person.

Credibility

- How much credibility do I have with this person?
- How do I know?
- How do they define credibility?
- How could I establish even greater credibility with them? What would it take?

Empathy

- What else can I do to pursue an understanding of their situation?
- To what extent am I likely to be perceived currently as having empathy?
- How am I demonstrating it?
- How do they know?
- Am I demonstrating it in a way they can relate to?

Logic

- How can I make my idea more palatable to the other person?
- What benefits would most appeal to them?
- Why?
- What reasons could they offer for not agreeing to the idea?
- How might I offer a 'reasoned' position with benefits to counter this?

SUMMARY

Some people are just better at persuasion, and now we have explored why and how that is possible. We've gone back as far as early Greece to track down the more powerful combination of actuating elements.

- Ethos—Personal credibility
- Pathos—Empathy
- Logos—Logical argument

Without trust and credibility, you are unlikely to get a fair hearing, so acting on the ideas in that section of this chapter will enable you to at least have your ideas listened to and considered.

Empathy is the next step in the process. The better you understand the other person and their unique perspective on things, the better your chances will be of putting a proposal together that attracts their attention and emotional interest. Put plainly, if the other person you are trying to connect with does not feel the similarity or emotional connection between you and them, or between their view of the world and yours—then the chances of persuasion occurring are slim to none.

Finally, we considered how to build a logical set of ideas into the proposition that will make sense to the other person and offer them things which they value as part of the package—including selecting the words you use carefully.

When efficiently used together, these three principles will make a world of difference to your success at persuasion.

REFLECT AND LEARN

What ideas from this chapter were novel, fresh or new to you? What learning was familiar? In what ways do you already apply some of this teaching?

How did you react emotionally and cognitively to the ideas in this chapter? What concepts do you agree with and why? What do you disagree with and why?

What were the most exciting or useful insights gained from reading and thinking about this chapter?

In what ways might you translate the ideas presented through this chapter into practical, useful, everyday ideas and plans?

What new questions about persuasion do you now have from reading this chapter?

ACTION LEARNING

In addition to the original three examples you selected at the beginning of the book, make a list of other people and situations where you could apply your learning on persuasion.

Set yourself some time-phased goals to apply some of the learning that you listed in the Reflect and Learn section. These goals should be chosen to guide your actions over the next three months, the next three weeks and the next three days.

Thinking about how you plan to apply your learning, what obstacles might you encounter along the way? Realistically, how might you deal with them?

Who else could you share these ideas with as a supportive sounding board or informal coach? How might you go about setting up a conversation with them to enrol them as a supporter of your application of this teaching? What might be some reasons they would consider for being involved? How might they also benefit?

3
Persuade—The Model

P E R S U A D E

Persuasion is a process that is dynamic, as each situation and each person is different. Although a person good at persuasion is intuitive and flexible, he/she is aware that having a framework for the way in which he/she approaches things will produce a better result than an erratic, unplanned approach.

- Thinking and planning before we try to persuade will avoid the 'open mouth and insert foot' human error
- This model will help you have more discipline to plan while enabling the flexibility to adapt
- Understanding and appealing to the other person's interests and motivators must be a central theme of all persuasion activities
- As you gain more knowledge and awareness of the other person, you'll find persuading becomes clearer and easier

Increase your influence and persuasiveness

- What **is it** that makes someone persuasive?
- **What** do they do that others don't?
- What is it that **separates them** from others?

These are tough questions indeed...

Someone today who can readily persuade and influence other people is probably someone who is more in demand today than ever before.

Because we are often hardened to the brutal assault of mass marketing and advertising by a plethora of media, more so today than ever before, we are naturally harder to be persuaded. We are more aware, more in tune, more cynical in a way.

Often in our quest to get our messages heard, it is sometimes worth remembering that less is more and simplicity in our approach can serve us well.

Everything should be made as simple as possible, but not simpler.

—Albert Einstein

So, let us look at a way we can keep our approach simple yet highly efficient, as we seek to persuade people.

So, what is persuasion?

To persuade someone efficiently, we must, in our approach, recognise the individual first, rather than our own argument or point of view.

A useful way to allow us to do this is to follow the PERSUADE model. This acronym is a sequential process that will enable us to test the integrity of our approach to influencing others.

As we go through this, think of someone you currently would like to influence or persuade and, using the wheel below, rate your own ability to win them over in each section as you read.

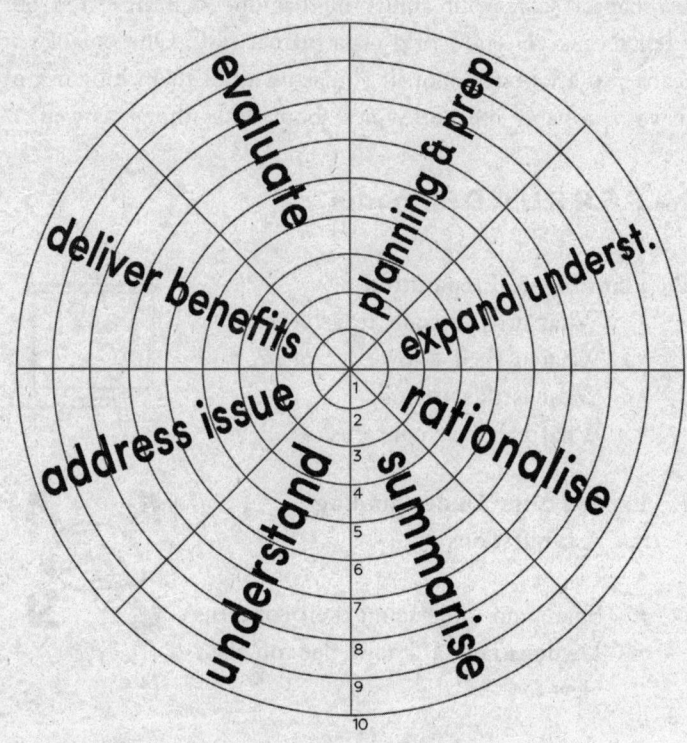

- P Planning & preparation
- E Expand your understanding
- R Rationalise
- S Summarise
- U Understand the person
- A Address/answer the issues
- D Deliver benefits
- E Evaluate outcome

Instructions

When you have finished reading each of the eight sections in this chapter score your ability in that one skill area. Ten out of ten means you are world class in that skill. One out of ten means you are pretty poor. If you score all of them nine out of ten you probably tell porky-pies about other things as well…

The P.E.R.S.U.A.D.E. model

P Planning & Preparation
- What do you want to achieve?
- What is their knowledge of it?
- What is their mood?
- What are their concerns?

E Expand Your Understanding
- Ask questions
- Listen
- Share and understand their concerns
- Demonstrate a knowledge of their view

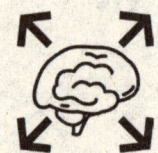

R Rationalise
- Use objective criteria
- Be clear about the issues
- Clarify key drivers, opportunities
- Clarify key benefits they would 'buy' into

S Summarise
- Demonstrate understanding of key issues
- Get agreement

U Understand the person
- Get agreement on the potential opportunity and potential benefits to be accrued
- Understand the person; consider style and approach

A Address/answer the issues
- Give answers
- Use facts and reasons
- Provide solutions

D Deliver benefits
- Use matching benefits
- Use FAB
- Connect to their needs, motivators in 'U'
- Use key drivers such as save, increase, improve, reduce, gain

E Evaluate outcome
- Check understanding
- Get clarity of common thinking

The P.E.R.S.U.A.D.E. model

Planning

In this section, we will review how we should stop, consider, and plan the best way we should approach someone when we wish to persuade them to act on something.

Aim

- To provide flexibility in our approach
- To decide the best approach for persuasion to achieve the desired results
- To determine the results we want to achieve

Should we be mindful of the perception our communication creates?

Of course we should. We want to be sure that we create the right perception, create the right feelings and stimulate the right course of action with someone we wish to persuade. Of course, whatever we do or say, or don't do or say, WILL create a perception. The truth is that it is not what we do with our communication that counts; it is what the other person does with it.

It is this very perception that will shape the success we have in our efforts to persuade. There are considerable benefits in thinking through and planning our communication in how we approach trying to convince someone. This is why we start with planning in our PERSUADE acronym.

Let's get started then.

From the three people you have identified you'd like to be more efficient at persuading at the start of this book, let's take one of those so we can see how this element of the PERSUADE model applies to them. Now that you have a person in your mind, we are going to use some considered thinking about how you go forward.

To start with, it is essential from the outset that you have a clear idea of what you want to achieve. All good plans begin with the end in mind. So take a moment to clarify your objective.

- Do you want them to DO something? If so, what?
- Do you want them to THINK differently? If so, how?

It might help if you consider their current perspective on the subject you are trying to persuade them on. What objective would seem reasonable for you to achieve with this person, bearing in mind where you think they are on this subject right now? This will help you decide the best approach.

Use the template below to capture your thoughts and initiate the thinking and planning process. Look at the example given and then use the blank template for your own.

Imagine, for example, I want to persuade a fictitious business colleague called Julie that the idea of having a team meeting on a Monday morning is a good idea. It is not Julie's decision but the manager's. I want to garner her support for the idea to get support from the whole team when I put it forward eventually at a team meeting.

My planning template might look like this:

Consideration	Your thoughts
What do they now know about the subject you want to persuade them on?	*I haven't raised the idea with them before. We have had meetings in the past, and I know Julie always enjoyed them. She knows that the team has changed over the past year, so I know she is aware of the benefit of team meetings and possibly the need to have one.*
Specifically, what is the best outcome?	*That she agrees with the idea, supports me on it in a group 'huddle' and that she is prepared to voice her own views as to why she thinks it is a good idea too.*
How will I measure it? How will I know I have achieved it?	*If she says to me face-to-face she agrees and is prepared to vocalise support when I raise it next week. Of course, I could then measure that she does indeed vocalise that support.*
What are the likely difficulties I may face with this person?	*She may think another day is better as I know she seems a whirlwind of activity on a Monday morning. Also, getting the time quietly for a few minutes to raise it.*
What do I know that they may find appealing about the subject?	*She's a great team player. Has always enjoyed past meetings. A chance for her to 'shine' with her results on recent projects.*

Consideration	Your thoughts
What do I want them to do? Take action? Think? Appreciate? Understand?	*Vocalise agreement to me. To vocalise support and agreement to others.*
What type of person are they? Slow and considered? Quick and excitable?	*She is quite chatty and fast paced. She 'flits' from one subject to the next so I need to be mindful of that. She is very caring and always happy to help others.*
How would you describe your present relationship with this person? Strong? Weak? Functional? Warm? Cool? Factual?	*I have worked with her for three-years and we get on well. We can talk about most things. We have had one or two minor disagreements in the past, but we have got over them the next day. I can always talk to her and would regard her as a good colleague/ maybe a friend.*

Now it's your turn—who is it you want to persuade?

Consideration	Your thoughts
What do they now know about the subject you want to persuade them on?	
Specifically, what is the best outcome?	
How will I measure it? How will I know I have achieved it?	
What are the likely difficulties I may face with this person?	

What do I know that they may find appealing about the subject?	
What do I want them to do? Take action? Think? Appreciate? Understand?	
What type of person are they? Slow and considered? Quick and excitable?	
How would you describe your present relationship with this person? Strong? Weak? Functional? Warm? Cool? Factual?	

- What history has gone before this?
- Are there likely to be objections?
- If so, what are they likely to be and what might cause them?
- How might you counter such concerns or objections?

Being able to manage the situation says as much about you as it does about the credibility of your message.

So how will planning the information in the grid help you?

- **Firstly:** It will stimulate your own thinking before you start the persuasion process. It will encourage ideas and thoughts that may not have been considered if you hadn't done this.
- **Secondly:** It gives you immense confidence in making the approach to that person. You are likely to have more success if you are seen and perceived as being confident

and you believe that your idea is a good one. Lack of planning can leave you feeling unsure as if you are on soft, flaky ground.
- **Thirdly:** It will help you decide what approach may work best, how you should make it and when. Communication must be tailored to the person as we are all unique. When God created you, he threw away the mould. So, it will help you decide how best to 'tailor' your approach to the person you wish to persuade.

This is about how you want to approach the person on the subject, bearing in mind much of the above. Is there something you need to consider regarding the climate and environment in which you intend to persuade?

Think also about you. Are you clear about what you want and precisely what you are trying to achieve? Do you want the other person to do something as a result, or do you want them to think differently? Are you in the right frame of mind? Are you ready to persuade with a positive 'we are both equal' mentality?

Planning will give you flexibility and credibility. It also helps give you the confidence to approach your influencing encounter from a favourable thinking window, where you feel you both have value and you are equals, not necessarily equals in position but equals in that you believe there are benefits you can offer this person. If you start your communication with them on a footing where you feel they are better than you, or you are better than they are (for whatever reason), then the approach, the style and the words will all be 'skewed' towards that thinking.

And that's not good...

So, let us move on and start to think about the person you are trying to persuade and to the second part of the PERSUADE acronym which is Expanding our understanding.

The P.E.R.S.U.A.D.E. model

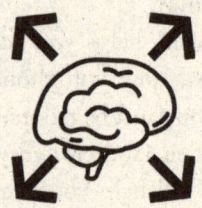

Expand your understanding

In this second part of the PERSUADE model, we will look at how understanding the person you wish to persuade better will help you to tailor your approach to suit them, thereby making your ideas more appealing to them, and more palatable in their eyes.

Aim

- To demonstrate empathy
- To understand what is important and what the critical issues are to them
- To build a solid foundation on which to build your persuasive case

Consider this question: Would you agree that the more you understand someone, the easier it is to persuade that individual to act on something?

Indeed, the more you understand them and how they see things, the more likely you are to know how to position your persuasive argument in a way that will make more sense to them. The more sense it makes, the more likely they will be to buy into it.

I don't care how much you know until I know how much you care.

Let us start with someone you have in mind who you would like to persuade. For this part of the PERSUADE acronym, you may wish to choose one of the other two people you considered at the beginning of this book—or if you want, you can continue with the same person.

The premise of being able to persuade someone to an idea or a course of action is knowing exactly what it will take to convince that person and how. Without it, it becomes a very challenging task indeed. We have already read in earlier chapters about how developing empathy is a critical ingredient in persuasion through the Greek philosophers, specifically Socrates.

Rapport and trust

The more rapport and trust you can instil in the person you wish to persuade, the greater your chances will be to increase your understanding of them. You need to determine what is important to them and what their key motivators are. So, what qualifies trust?

Integrity—is established if you are seen and perceived as a person of character, and that your behaviour reflects good morals and values. Remember, people judge us on our actions, not our intentions. Yet we judge ourselves on our intentions. The fact that you are perceived as someone who is honest, principled, believes in a sense of fair play, has a firm belief in what is right or wrong and, above all, is prepared to act on those ideas. Can you answer the following questions positively?

- Does my behaviour reflect my beliefs?
- Am I genuine in my feedback?
- Am I likely to be regarded as two-faced?

In your own view with the person you have in mind—how would they rate your integrity?

Competence—is it a fact that the other person believes you to be competent in your relationship with them and you express proficiency in your working role and in your ability to deliver results for the business?

Outside of the role, competence could well be the fact that the other person believes you to be competent on a more social level with them. This is achieved by:

- Listening
- Giving feedback
- Doing what you say you will do
- Keeping promises
- Being reliable (including—can you keep a secret?)

Compassion—This is about caring, but also being seen to care. In fact, compassion can be summed up as:

- Caring and taking a genuine interest
- Being seen to care and take a real interest
- Being seen to act sensitively with consideration and feeling

The more you believe that someone has a genuine interest in you, the more it will demonstrate that they appreciate your point of view or predicament. The other person's behaviour will go on to reflect that, and this will create a stronger sense of trust with that person. Caring internally doesn't count, because if it isn't outwardly displayed, then what is the other person likely to think?

- He/She doesn't care?
- He/She doesn't listen?
- He/She doesn't understand?

None of these may be true, but as we discussed earlier, people judge us on our actions, not our intentions.

> **Quick activity**
>
> - How would *you* rate your trust in this person?
>
> - How would *they* rate their trust in you?
>
> - What one thing could you do to improve the level of mutual trust you share?

Seek first to understand before you seek to be understood.
—Dr Stephen Covey

Iceberg

Human behaviour has, for some time, been compared to an iceberg. Why? Because with an iceberg, only a small part of it is visible above the water. Let's say that there is no more than 10% visible. Just because we cannot see the other 90% doesn't mean that it doesn't exist.

Well, the same applies to trust and how we communicate it to others. Some things about our persona are visible and conspicuous (that's our 10% by the way). What might they be?

- Our words are evident as they can be heard instantly
- Our tone that is used with the words can be picked up straight away
- Our body language is evident as it can be seen immediately

Are the words we choose to use, and the body language we demonstrate, in any way reflected by the person we are talking to and how we feel about that relationship?

Almost certainly... In fact, what drives our 10% is what is going on below the water in the lower part of the iceberg. Things below the water that are not visible to the other person may be:

- Attitude
- Opinions
- Experience
- Knowledge
- Emotions
- Hopes
- Fears
- Feelings

There are of course others, but we can see that what someone may be feeling, or their opinion of the discussion subject or the other person will have an impact on the behaviour and words demonstrated—the 10% above the water that IS visible.

So, in the pursuit of expanding my understanding of this

person, I may well want to find out more about their iceberg. In other words, I may well want to find out more about their experiences on a subject, their feelings on a matter or their knowledge on a topic.

> **Quick activity**
>
> - Draw an iceberg on a piece of paper for the person you would like to persuade. Write the parts in the 10% and the elements below the water.
> - Which one element below the water would you gain most value from in learning more about in order to help understand them?
> - Write down three things you could do in the next two weeks to give you a better understanding of that element.

What are the areas I wish to know more about?

Rather than just gaining a general understanding of the other person, it will be more advantageous to you to consider specific areas where it would be useful to gain a better understanding of them. Why do you need to obtain more information in specific areas and how do you know what areas they may be?

The reason for wanting to gain a better understanding of specific areas of others is that this will provide you with more information that will help to build your case of persuasion with my fictitious colleague Julie. If we take a step back, you will remember that I wanted to persuade her to accept that having a meeting on a Monday morning was a good idea. In the case of Julie, there are one or two areas more than others where I would undoubtedly like to gain a better understanding of her point of view.

In Julie's example, all the areas are essential as they will undoubtedly be relevant in some way to the case of persuading her that having Monday meetings is beneficial.

Monday mornings—If, for example, she usually has a hectic Monday morning due to the way she organises her workload, then that will have a strong bearing on HOW I position my proposition of having a Monday meeting.

Weekends—Maybe she goes away at weekends and arrives back very late Sunday night. She may, if that is true, not necessarily welcome a Monday meeting with open arms.

Her experiences of meetings in the past—If I knew she has always had a great experience of meeting in the past, then I would be well placed to sell the benefits to her more easily. If, however, she has had poor experiences in the past, then I would need to consider very carefully how best to persuade her why meeting on a Monday morning is such a good idea.

Her view on meetings—Does she think meetings generally are a waste of time? Does she think we have too many? Does she think we have too few? All will be factors in the timing and method of my approach to her.

Her view on team building—Perhaps she thinks we don't get together enough as a team? Does she genuinely value the team effort? Does she like the camaraderie of the team and the *esprit de corps*? In other words, how essential are these elements to her and could/should they be used in my attempts to persuade her?

Results—Does she always have her eye on her individual results, the team results and the business results? What level of importance does she place on these?

So far, in expanding our understanding, we have considered what we may know already and what the areas where having a better knowledge would help. Now what we need to look at are the types of questions in these areas that will help bring about the best form of understanding.

Asking questions

Asking questions will help enable you to:

- Try and understand the other person's current understanding of a subject
- Determine what their views and perspective on things is likely to be
- Discover what sorts of things are important to them
- Find out what their motivators are
- Learn the needs they are trying to satisfy. In other words, discover what is important to them

The reason for asking the person you are trying to persuade questions is because:

- It is a common courtesy
- It helps create and build empathy essential for your ability to persuade
- It will help you position your logic and your argument if you are to be able to persuade the other person more easily

The person you are trying to persuade will be much more likely to listen to you if you can demonstrate that you are prepared to listen to them and understand.

> *The best way to persuade people is with your ears—by listening to them.*
>
> —Dean Rusk

You don't want to appear contrived in trying to gain a better understanding by clinically planning questions that seem to care little about the person. It is better to have given thought to the general direction of your questions, so when you ask them it feels like they fit together, flow naturally, show respect and have a purpose. That has surely got to be more effective than rambling through a conversation aimlessly which achieves very little and / or shows disrespect to the other person.

> *If you would persuade, you must appeal to interest rather than intellect.*
>
> —Dwight D. Eisenhower (1890–1969)
> 34th President of the USA

Open and closed questions

Much has been said and written about open versus closed questions, and I certainly am not going to shed anything new on them today. However, I am likely to use both in my conversation with my fictitious colleague Julie.

At the risk of covering ground many readers will know intimately, I would like to re-establish the purpose of both open and closed questions.

- General open question—to gain general information
- Specific open question—to gain information in a specific area
- Closed question—to gain confirmation to a point

Let us now look at the type of questions I may wish to consider in my conversation with my fictitious colleague Julie. Again, these are the areas where I want to expand my understanding of the arguments she may introduce. The following are questions that I will ask her:

Her typical schedule on a Monday morning
How do you set yourself up for the week?
Are Mondays vital to you in achieving what you want in the week?
Do you find Mondays are busier than other days?

Weekend activities
What do you get up to over the weekend?
Are you like me in that you tend to cram loads of things into weekends?
Do you find Monday mornings feeling as if you need another weekend?

Her experience of meetings in the past
What's the best/worst meeting you have ever been to?
What (in your view) makes a meeting worthwhile?
What's your biggest hope/fear in meetings?
If you were chairing a meeting, what would you be sure to do/avoid?

Her views on the value of meetings and the role they play
Should we have meetings in our department?
How should we feel going into and coming out of a meeting?

Her view on teambuilding and teamwork
How would you describe our team/department?
What do you think of what we have done in the past with regard to team development?
I think team development is an ongoing process—what do you think?

Where she is regarding results; how important she thinks results are
How are you getting on this month/quarter?
You seem to take responsibility for your objectives—how do you keep them at the front of your mind?
What might help you achieve more?

Let's assume for a moment that for the past week or two I have investigated deeper into these areas and I have now learned the following about my fictitious colleague Julie.

Area of understanding	What do I now know?
Weekend activities	Very little other than time with her child. She seems to go shopping on Saturdays and spend time with her family on Sunday. She generally arrives late, although occasionally on time, because she takes her child to school. She seems to have a lot to tend to, and I now know that on a Monday morning she plans her week in detail to give herself a goal, follows up calls from last week and reorganises her desk.
Her experience of meetings in the past	She seems to like the idea of meetings—but only if done well. She has sat in too many that seem to go on for too long, or where she felt she didn't need to be there.

Area of understanding	What do I now know?
Her view on the value of meetings and the role they play	The general idea is a good one according to Julie, but she says, "They are like a gun, in that in the wrong hands they are dangerous!"
Her view on teambuilding and teamwork	Pretty much as above but feels they can be handy and should be an essential part of team development. She seems to be all for them, although her experiences have somewhat tarnished her view. Excellent idea—essential. She remembers the teambuilding weekend vividly that we did two-years ago and said it was one of the most memorable of her working career.
Where she is regarding results, and how important she thinks results are	Results in her job are critical. She said that having some time Monday morning helps her focus and organise her thoughts for the week ahead. She knows she can be 'scatty' (her word) and unless she gets that 'focus' she will never be able to focus. She is performing currently at 97.5% effectiveness against her goals and objectives for the quarter.

Now let's turn to you. Think about the person that you started with at the beginning of this book (or someone else if you prefer) and think about the area where you could gain a better understanding and the type of question you could ask in that area:

Area of understanding	Questions you could ask

The P.E.R.S.U.A.D.E. model

Rationalise

Having come this far, I have thought much about how I wish to approach my fictitious colleague Julie. I have also taken the time to find out and learn more about her and have expanded my understanding of specific issues.

A lot of information has been identified, but not all of it may be relevant. So, in this part of the PERSUADE acronym, I am looking to identify which areas are essential so that I will be most able to rationalise the information objectively.

Aim

- To understand the issues
- To objectively clarify the other person's principal drivers, needs and motivators

In your own case scenario, from all the information, thought and feelings you have gathered, what does the person you are trying to persuade consider to be the critical issues? It is essential to clarify these issues so that they can be used as objective criteria in forming the basis of the persuasion.

Can you clarify the drivers that are important to the other person? Factors such as increase, gain, improve, reduce and save. Also, what key benefits are vital to them and are likely to appeal to them? To rationalise, you are seeking to simplify and therefore clarify.

In my dealings with Julie, the following are fundamental questions I want to ask myself:

- What are the critical issues to her?
- What is negotiable and what is not?
- What are the cold hard facts?

In my example with my fictitious colleague Julie the key issues that are regarded as very important to her are:

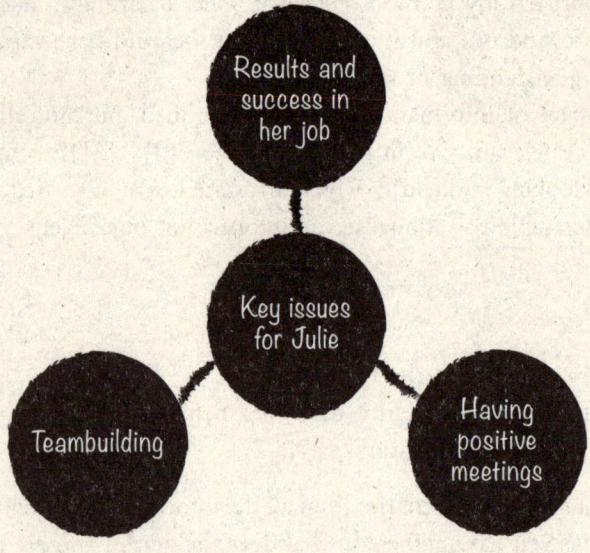

It is with this understanding that I will build my case in trying to persuade Julie that having a meeting on a Monday morning is a good idea.

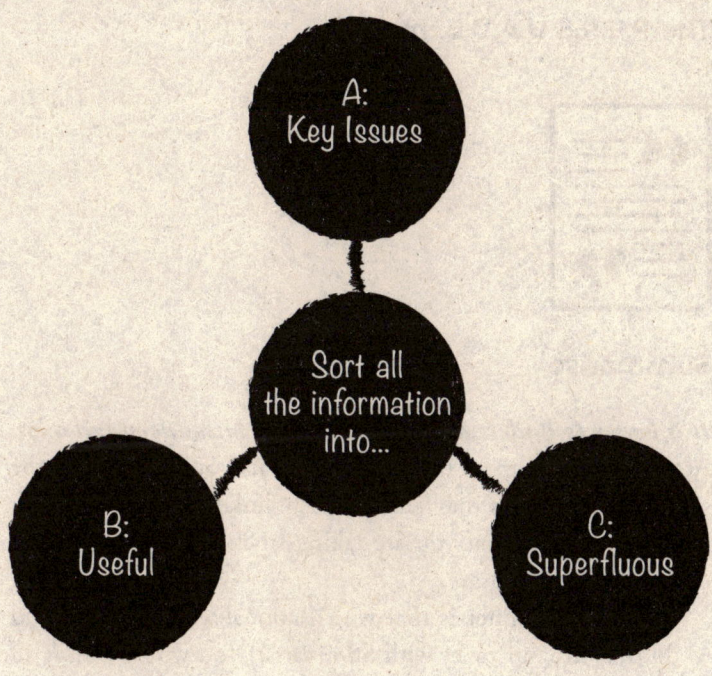

Quick activity

- What are the benefits in Rationalising?
- Find yourself some time and space and jot down all the information you know about the person you wish to persuade.
- Sort the information into three groups using the model above if you wish.

The P.E.R.S.U.A.D.E. model

Summarise

It is better to understand a little than to misunderstand a lot.
At first it may appear that Rationalise and Summarise are the same. In some ways they are obviously linked, as they are both in 'stop' mode in that you are taking stock and having a sense check of where you are.

Where they differ is that with Rationalise you would tend to do this on your own; with Summarise, you would pull it all together in your head before finding an appropriate time to say it to / discuss it with the person you are seeking to persuade, in my case my fictitious colleague Julie. Remember, the aim of this section is:

Aim

- To achieve a mutual understanding

With Summarising, I am not only identifying the critical issues, but I am also clarifying:

- The key points
- What has been said
- What is not being said and possibly inferred

- Their feelings and emotions on a topic
- Their motivators
- Their aims and hopes
- Their fears

It is in the strictest sense a short, accurate statement that reflects:

- Where that person is now in relation to the subject at hand
- Their journey/experience in the past
- How they'd like to see things

So with regard to my fictitious colleague Julie, based on the information I have gained, I might summarise the situation as:

"Julie is a whirlwind of activity and really needs to stay focused to achieve results which are very important to her. Her bad experiences of meetings in the past tarnish her view of the value of any future meetings. Having said that, she would like to continue with them as I guess she feels they will help her and the team spirit."

Before even considering approaching Julie with my idea, I would pick the right time and moment to 'playback' to her how I think she sees the situation:

"Julie, I know you haven't had great experiences of meetings in the past—despite the fact you think the idea is generally a good one. I guess what you're saying is that if they added value and helped with results you'd be more for it—is that about it?

It is crucial for you to demonstrate an understanding of the critical issues and get an agreement on them. The more you can recap on what you both agree are the main issues, the more robustly your persuasion will stand as it is clearly seeking to influence issues that are seen as essential.

This also makes sure that you both approach your argument with the same level of understanding.

> **Quick activity**
>
> - What elements of building a relationship does summarising help with?
> - What symptoms of a breakdown in communication could occur if there is no use of summarising to confirm a mutual understanding?
> - Where and when could you summarise in a conversation with the person you wish to persuade?

The P.E.R.S.U.A.D.E. model

Understand the person

> *There is nothing so unequal as the equal treatment of unequals.*
>
> —Ken Blanchard

Given the fact that we are all different, it goes without saying that we all interpret things in different ways. If two people witnessed the same incident from a window, for example, and both are asked to recall what they saw, they would each recall things differently, with different details and possibly in a different order. Remember that we are all complex creatures and devour information and are persuaded in a variety of ways.

Because we all take information in differently and recall things differently, it is sensible to think about the person, rather than just the message, at this point. In this section, we are going to consider how we do all vary, and specifically, how the person you wish to persuade is not likely to be the same as you. The fact that we are different will influence the way you approach them.

Aim

- To be able to position your proposition so that it makes sense and is appealing to the person you wish to persuade
- For the other person to receive your approach in the way it is intended

Let's think about personality styles when dealing with other people. Do they take information in slowly or with speed? Are they quick to react or slow to respond? Do they talk facts or feelings? Understanding the person will give you reliable clues about what to present, when to persuade, why you are persuading and, more importantly, **how** to present your argument of persuasion.

Some people relate to words—some people prefer pictures or visual support. Some people need more background information—some people merely want the facts. Some people like you to show support and care—others want you to merely get to the point! Some people want you to 'sell the sausage'—others just the sizzle. So we need to understand the person as an individual.

The apostle Paul was a great persuader who always considered the background and thinking of his listeners when persuading. "I have become all things to people of all sorts," he said. He was very adaptable.

Although we have sought to expand our understanding of the person's views on things in the 'E' section of PERSUADE covered earlier in the book, we are now going to consider elements of the personal style of the prospect you are aiming to influence. To do this, consider in your mind someone you wish to persuade on something in the future. You can, of course, use the same person you have been thinking of earlier, or you may want to find someone else. Again, I will use my fictitious colleague Julie in the process.

To illustrate how personal styles differ, let us consider an activity that I will encourage you to do as we proceed. In this process, I will ask you to draw some lines (so you should have a piece of paper and a pen to hand). I will also be asking you to assess where you think your person is against some criteria that I will ask you to consider.

Firstly, draw a vertical line on the piece of paper you have in front of you and make five demarcation points so that it looks like this:

Persuade—The Model

Let us assume that the dot at the top is a measure of people orientation and the dot at the bottom is a measure of task orientation. **People orientation** means the degree to which a person shows people-oriented tendencies. These might include listening, praise, support, giving feedback, encouragement and rapport building, among others.

Task orientation means the degree to which a person shows concern for the task. Task-oriented tendencies can be goals, objectives, to-do lists, focussing on the time and achievements.

Although there are only five dots, I'd like you to consider where you think the person you have in mind can be placed on this line. It's not meant to be an exact science, just where you think they are. Which dot do you feel they are closest to? You'll no doubt find that your prospect will show a mix of both people and task tendency, but you need to consider which they demonstrate more of. As a result, mark on the line where you think they are. In my case, let me take my fictitious colleague Julie. Although she can be quite chatty and is friendly, she is increasingly concerned about personal results and the team's results, so, on reflection, I will put Julie here:

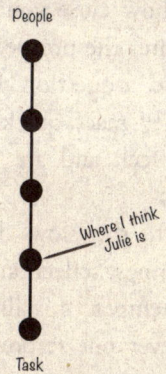

Now draw another line, this time horizontally, that crosses the centre of the vertical line, like so:

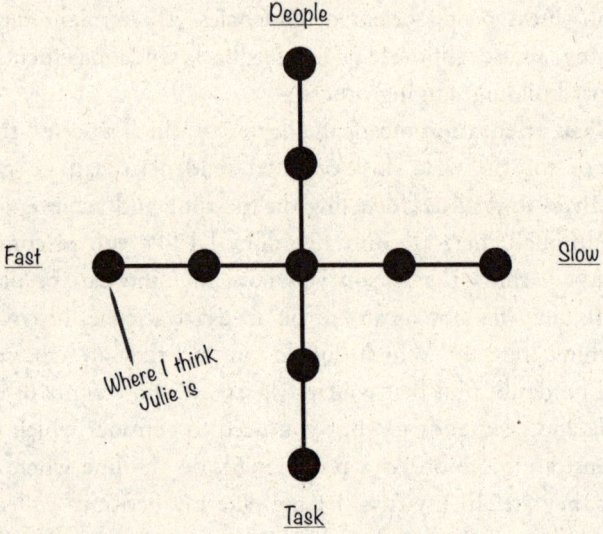

On this horizontal line, write 'fast' on the left and 'slow' on the right. Placing the dot in between fast and slow will be a mix of both, depending on how close you are to the final dot at the edge. This line measures the prospect's speed of response to any stimulus, for example, a question. If your prospect is close to the fast dot, then they react quickly, are likely to answer questions based on gut feel, and are very expressive verbally and with body language.

If someone is close to the 'slow' dot, then they are more measured, think about things, reflect, and are less likely to react at all immediately. Remember, this line measures merely the speed of reaction—not everyone responds to a situation at the same rate.

Now indicate where on the line you think the person you wish to persuade is likely to be. Which dot do you think they will be closest to?

Considering my fictitious colleague Julie, I know from my earlier observations that she is 'fast-paced and chatty'. This provides me with sufficient evidence to know where I would put her!

So what does all this tell us?

Well, we can see that our two intersecting lines have created four quadrants (fast/people, fast/task, slow/people, slow/task) and each quadrant represents an easy-to-identify personality trait. To make it easier to understand and for ease of identification, I will give each quadrant a title:

- Fast/Task—Driver
- Fast/People—Expressive
- Slow/Task—Analytical
- Slow/People—Amiable

It is wise to remember that everyone has a mix of all four styles in their character. Most people have a primary style and as such will display behaviours, traits or characteristics of one kind more than others.

The closer you place someone to the middle, at the point where the vertical and horizontal lines intersect, the more likely they are to display a personality style that is very flexible and adaptable. The more that individual is put towards the far edge of that quadrant in the white space, the more they are likely to display behaviours of that kind, and the more comfortable they are with that style.

> **Quick activity**
>
> - How would you describe the type of people you get on with best?
> - What's the best way for someone to persuade you?

In PERSUADE, let us continue with our journey in the 'U' section that will help you to understand the person. You are trying to understand something about the personality of the person you wish to persuade and how best you can communicate with them effectively. So, now that you have understood where that person is located within the four quadrants, let's move on and plan the style that would work best when trying to persuade them. I know now that my fictitious colleague Julie is Fast/Task—Driver, so I will be considering that as we look at each personality trait in sequence.

I will begin by looking at behaviours that are generally associated with each style.

Style	How to identify them
Driver	• Focussed on goals and objectives • Works quickly and to the point • Can be described as blunt, daring, forceful • Definite behaviour and wording • Quick reactor and need accomplishment • Can see rules as a barrier
Expressive	• Outgoing and gregarious • Works well with people • Digresses very easily • Excitable and enthusiastic • Likes rapport, banter and the 'craic'

Style	How to identify them
Analytical	• Slow to react • Careful and considered • Decisions are made slowly, based on fact, proof and evidence • Accuracy is the key motivator • Often described as precise, guarded and reflective
Amiable	• Good listener • Kind and considerate • Motivated by stability • Values relationships of trust, openness and honesty • Hates being rushed • Reluctant to decide—would prefer to 'go along' with everyone else • Careful, considered and considerate

Can you see characteristics in your prospect from the grid above based on your initial thinking? Out of interest, which style are you?

Where are the points of difference?

The two styles at the opposite end of each axis will present the biggest challenge to each other's personalities. For example, a Driver would find it difficult persuading an Amiable person because their personality traits are opposed on both the pace axis and the focus axis. An Expressive subject would face a considerable challenge convincing an individual who is an Analytical for the very same reasons.

- Analyticals and Drivers share the **Focus** axis
- Analyticals and Amiable share the **Pace** axis
- Amiable and Expressives share the **Focus** axis
- Expressives and Drivers share the **Pace** axis

What factors could contribute towards persuading each style?

If the person you are aiming to persuade is **Analytical**, then consider:

- Giving them time to make a decision—don't rush them
- Providing them with all the facts, reasons and evidence to make their decision making easier
- Approaching them calmly and in a considered way
- Giving them the background to your reasoning—your thinking behind it
- Explaining the risks or pitfalls in 1) going with your decision, and 2) not going with your decision
- Being well prepared by having all the relevant information ready, whether written or in your head

If the person you are aiming to persuade is an **Amiable**, then consider:

- Giving them time to make a decision, don't rush them
- Pointing out why this may be good for the team
- Demonstrating how such a decision is relatively safe, and not too radical
- Using your own relationship with the person to convey your message. Use the trust and honesty you already have by expressing that YOU think it's a good idea and by showing you wouldn't suggest something to them if

you didn't believe it to be a good idea.
- Introducing the subject/proposal gently—by not making it look too contrived

If the person you are aiming to persuade is a **Driver**, then consider:

- Being prepared by having all the facts
- Showing how making a decision will have a positive impact on results
- Getting to the point quickly. They are likely to want to know what is it, why should they do it, how much does it cost and what do they get?
- Avoiding too much small talk and 'subjectivity' by keeping to objectivity

If the person you are aiming to persuade is an **Expressive**, then consider:

- That they value energy, enthusiasm and excitement—so be enthusiastic!
- Showing images if you have them or describing things in a visual way
- Painting the big picture—how it will look in the future
- Keeping the pace moving briskly
- Probably not offering too much detail

Now is the time to consider what style your person is? Think back to the manner they used when they most often communicated with you. If you think they are brisk and to the point, then they may be 'Drivers'. If you think they are very considered and tend to mull things over, then they may either be 'Analytical' or 'Amiable', depending on other behaviours or traits.

For me, considering my fictitious colleague Julie, I know

from my earlier observation that she is 'fast-paced and chatty' which points to the Expressive style. However, I know she is far more concerned with the task at hand, so I would say this will make her **more** of a Driver.

Now, think of the person you wish to persuade and consider how you would respond to the following:

- Are they fast or slow in the way they generally respond?
- Are they excitable?
- Do they show enthusiasm and energy?
- Do they delve into detail, facts and figures?
- Are they supportive?
- Do they make decisions quickly?
- Are they thoughtful, careful and considered?
- How would they feel if they upset you or someone else on the team?

Having done this, you should now be in a better position to identify the style of your prospect to help you **understand the person** in the PERSUADE acronym. This will be useful to bear in mind as we move on through the next few chapters of the book and deal with ways to approach your prospect.

The P.E.R.S.U.A.D.E. model

Address the issues

Aim

- To ensure your proposition 'hits home' in that it addresses the issues that have been identified earlier
- To provide solutions or opportunities

If I didn't have to address the issues, I would merely put my idea forward for a Monday morning meeting because that is what I want to do. But of course, for my opinion to be more readily accepted, I need to garner support first. My issues have to be seen as having a connection to the problems of the person I aim to persuade. So when we talk about issues, they are more likely to be issues related to the person you seek to influence.

Firstly, what are issues? Issues are any points that have been identified that need to be addressed in the persuasion process. These are likely to be concerns for the person you wish to persuade, and they could well be issues that you too want dealt with in the process.

The point about the persuasion process is that the issues are identified and recognised and that the proposal you put forward directly addresses those issues (in my case you may remember it is persuading my fictitious colleague Julie that having a team meeting on a Monday morning is a good idea). In other words, I must demonstrate how my concept has a direct positive impact on the issues I know about for the person I wish to persuade.

> **Quick activity**
>
> - When you last persuaded someone successfully, what did you do?
> - When someone tries to persuade you, what works and doesn't work? What puts you off? Annoys you?

Secondly, what are the issues concerning my fictitious colleague?

- She's a 'Driver', so I need to be focussed on results and get to the point
- Despite being a 'Driver', she is also a great team player and would welcome a new forum to show her results on recent projects
- She's a whirlwind of activity so keeping her attention will be key
- Monday mornings are crucial to her. I need to bear this in mind for pitching the idea of a Monday meeting
- When would the best approach be to actually raise my plan with her? Monday morning? Probably not...
- Results are key to her
- She is currently performing at 97.5% of her target, so I know she is focussed on making up the remaining 2.5%
- She thinks meetings are a good idea, although I need to be mindful in my approach because she has had poor past experiences

> **Think of the person you wish to persuade:**
> What are the issues for them?
> -
> -
> -
> -
> -
> -
> -
> -
> -
> -

So, coming back to Julie, how would having a team meeting on a Monday morning help address one of more of these issues? It could be that having the meeting will enable Julie to enjoy:

- More of something
- Less of something

I also want to think whether the idea of a meeting could help Julie to:

- Move closer to something
- Move away and distance her from something

What things might come into play here that Julie might appreciate less or more?

- Results
- Planning time
- Stress
- Personal motivation
- Team spirit
- Wasted time
- Personal organisation

Think about this for a moment. Would Julie perceive the idea of having a team meeting on a Monday morning to be giving her less or more of the following?

Idea—Monday morning meeting

Issue	More/Closer	Less/Further away
Results	More focussed. Better chance of finding that missing 2.5%	Reduce missed opportunities
Planning time	Spread her desire to use Monday morning to clear the decks and plan the week across the team	Reduce conflicting priorities
Stress	Improve the sharing of the workload	Less last-minute dot com
Personal motivation	A regular opportunity to review progress and plan goals	Reduce the frustrations from having too much to do herself
Team spirit	Better communication, calibration and harmony across the team	Remove friction caused by lack of shared understanding
Wasted time	Work done on the important goals and tasks	Reduce the negative impact of the whirlwind on the team's activities
Personal organisation	More organised	Be less scatty

As we can see, addressing the issues may promote the idea of the person you are trying to persuade gaining either less or more of something. Either way, these factors could determine whether or not the prospect can be persuaded towards your way of thinking. Obviously, to know whether a specific factor in the sequence of persuasion will attract your prospect, you first have to know the person and understand what is important to them. This subject was approached earlier in the book in the section 'Expand your understanding'.

Now, turn back to the prospect you have in mind that you wish to persuade.

a) List the known, or suspected, issues in the left-hand column of the table below as I have done in the example above
b) Add the ideas you wish to use to persuade your prospect in the 'More' column
c) Next, measure your ideas against each of those from the perspective of your prospect in the right-hand column. How would they see it?

Your Idea is:

Issue	More/Closer	Less/Further away

Issue	More/Closer	Less/Further away

In summary, consider how you intend to address the issues that are on the other person's mind and when you will do it. Give facts and reasons. Be rational and logical. Ensure that the majority of what you say hits on the issues that they regard as significant. Seek to demonstrate how you can satisfy the critical issues that are important to the person you wish to persuade. Remember the lessons from the earlier chapter on the Basis of Persuasion, especially the three Greek Amigos, Ethos, Pathos and Logos.

Make sure you are able to demonstrate how what you are

saying will connect and influence the issues that are important. Do not leave it to your prospect to work things out for themselves—because they won't!

The P.E.R.S.U.A.D.E. model

Deliver Benefits

Aim

- To raise buying desire and facilitate the 'buy-in' process
- To demonstrate empathy

What is the difference between addressing the issues and delivering benefits? As the celebrated Irish comedian, Frank Carson, might say, "It's the way I tell 'em". Addressing the issues is fine if we are sure the reasoning is rational, logical and well matched. To Deliver Benefits, we consider how we verbalise and express these to the person we wish to persuade. In this section of PERSUADE we are concerned with the language and wording we must use to influence the other person. We want to use persuasive communication, and with this in mind, we must ensure that our language and phraseology contain lots of benefits.

Chinese Proverb:
That which proves too much, proves nothing!

What do we mean by benefits?

Benefits are the parts and aspects of our proposition (from when we addressed the issues) which help, assist and benefit the other person in some way. Naturally, we want to make sure we offer the right benefits—those that have the most appeal, rather than just depending on random benefits that have no real meaning to the prospect at that time. Care must be taken to ensure that the words that we use will appeal to the other person's interest.

Why do we need to use benefits?

Benefits, when used in the correct terminology to best suit the person we wish to persuade, are the lynchpin to them acting in line with our idea. If we use benefits that appeal to the desires, needs or wants of the other person, we are offering valid reasons (to them) that hopefully present a sensible argument to convince them to want to do what we are asking.

We deliberately use benefits to appeal to the other person to motivate them to act to conform with our wishes. What we are doing is giving them positive reasons to do it for them, rather than reasons to do it for us. Without our use of benefits, our argument will lack the compelling reasons for the other person to be persuaded.

Quick activity

When you last persuaded someone successfully, what benefits did you use? Why do you think you were successful in persuading them?

Think back to when someone persuaded you to do something. Why did you do it? What benefits did you see?

How do we use benefits?

Don't sell what it is—sell what it does!
When presenting your reasons using facts and logic, be sure to maximise the appeal to the other party by converting what you are proposing into benefits to them. This conversion process, or conversion mechanism, often involves words or phrases such as:

- "Which means that ..."
- "What this means to you is ..."
- "This will mean ..."
- "Therefore ..."

For example:

"I'd like to suggest we start our meeting 30 minutes earlier."
(Logic and reasoning)

"This will mean that you can have more time to debate the issues at the end of the meeting which I know is something you are very keen to do."
(Benefit)

The more you deliver benefits, the more you are influencing 'buying desire' because what you connect to has a direct correlation to something that the prospect cares about. Let us consider some other examples.

Each of the statements below has no benefits attached. They are merely features or statements of fact. If you had chosen to use one, some or all of these in the process of persuading someone for whatever reason, you would need to be sure that they are phrased correctly. This would include using benefits to appeal to something that is of interest to the other person. Of course, in real life, it will depend on the person and the situation, but for now, let us make some assumptions about the way you should convert the statements below into benefits.

Take a look; can you see some obvious benefits that could be attached to each?

- The printer prints 35 pages a minute
- We offer a money-back guarantee
- We offer a delivery service to your door

Of course, the benefits you place on each will depend on the person you wish to persuade and what appeals to them. But, let us consider some generic examples and how these can be converted into benefits.

- **The printer prints 35 pages a minute** which means that (convert) you can get the job done quicker saving you time and helping you to be more efficient (benefit).
- **We offer a money-back guarantee**—therefore (convert) if for whatever reason you are unhappy with the product, you can bring it back. Consequently, you can shop with total peace of mind (benefit).
- **We offer a delivery service to your door**—meaning (convert) that you don't have any of the hassle of getting to and from the shop, so you can relax (benefit) and avoid any disruption to your day. This means you can get on with more of the things you want to (benefit).

So, when we offer something devised to persuade, it is essential for it:

- To be relevant and logical to the other person
- To have a 'conversion mechanism'
- To be worded positively in beneficial terms that will have the most appeal to the other person

Returning to my fictitious colleague Julie for a moment, I now need to consider which benefits would have the most appeal to her.

- More results
- More planning time
- Less stress
- More personal motivation
- Better team spirit
- Less wasted time
- More personal organisation

I need to package the above list into a series of statements that combine the logical rationale and the benefits to her.

Context	"Julie, I know how busy and focused you are, and how getting results is key to you. Like you, being successful is important to me as well. It's a harsh old world and doing this and staying motivated isn't easy. "I've been thinking about an idea that will help..."
Lead in	"I've been thinking about what you've been saying to me over the past week or two, and I've got an idea about how we can approach team meetings. While we've not always been good at them in the past, I think there is a great opportunity to improve results and I wondered if I can run this by you?"
Benefit	"This idea, I believe, will help us stay more focussed and have an even better chance of getting the results we want—not only that, but probably be even more organised."

Proposal	"My idea is that it would be really worthwhile to have a Monday morning team meeting, Julie. I am aware of your own experiences of meetings, but if they are managed well, this could have a huge influence over results in a way that could really help us."
Benefit	"It wouldn't impact on your own planning time and is even likely to enhance it. We could make the focus of the meeting about how we are all managing to achieve results, and we could use the meeting as a brainstorming forum that would help us all. We could also use it to help understand each other better and how everyone is using their time, so we can work better with each other to make sure we all get the planning time we individually want."
Feedback	"We all start work at 9.00am so my idea is we start the meeting at 9.15am for 25 minutes. Enough time to focus on goals and ideas, but not too long to have any negative effect on the achievement of one's day. "In fact, the more I think about it, I believe it will help us all (I know it will help me!) to be less stressed as we will feel more in control and therefore even more motivated. "What do you think Julie?"

If you notice, with Julie, I am doing several things:

- I am offering two sets of benefits.
- I am providing benefits 'before' the idea and benefits after the idea.

- I am making clear my idea.
- I am connecting my idea to several benefits that will appeal to Julie, not relying on just a single benefit.
- I am making it appear to Julie that the concept is sound, reasonable and logical.
- I am making it seem that there are more reasons to do it than not to do it.
- I am alternating the use of 'We' and 'You'. I am keen to impress the benefits she will gain, but equally share the fact that, as her friend, I will benefit and so too will the team.
- I am using the word 'you' as often as I can and the word 'I' less frequently—without making my sentences clumsy or sound overly contrived.
- I am showing that my idea has been well considered and clearly thought through. Why? Because, if it is perceived and believed that one's idea has been carefully considered and thought through, it will be taken far more seriously than something off the top of one's head.

Of course, it is not guaranteed to have instant success. If we all had a formula for that, I wouldn't be writing this book, and you wouldn't be reading it! However, using benefit statements in this way is likely to dramatically increase your chances of success in persuading anyone to accept your idea.

Be prepared for their initial response

In the planning stage to gaining acceptance of my idea, I would have needed to consider what Julie's likely response would be to such a proposal. It is expected she would act instinctively at first as she is fast paced. She may say:

- "Do you really think it will work?"
- "What makes you think this will be any different from other meetings?"
- "Do we have the time—aren't we busy enough?"

She could say other things too, of course, but I dare say these are the three questions she would most likely ask. What is important here is that I have anticipated the kind of reactions I am most likely to get from Julie. I have also thought of empathetic responses that I can make that will help reassure her that the idea I am putting to her is a good one.

"Do you really think it will work?"
"Well, that's a good point, Julie, because that was one of my first thoughts. If we manage the process, content and timing well, I think it will work better than we might anticipate."

"What makes you think this meeting will be any different from others?"
"Yes, that's the big worry, isn't it? Certainly, if they were the same I wouldn't be interested. The difference in my mind is the focus of this meeting; we publish a finish time (not just a start time!), and we collectively take responsibility for making it work—it's **our** meeting."

"Do we have the time—aren't we busy enough?"
"That's an excellent point. In my mind Julie, it will help create more time, as after the 25 minutes we become more focused and can get on with the day even quicker. Not only that, most of us would spend some time doing the things we can do far better in a more focused and highly-motivating 20 to 25 minutes.

I suppose it is also because we are so busy that we'd want to be sure we can compress some activities and therefore make the best use of time."

So, thinking about the person that you wish to persuade, take some time to consider the following. Firstly, bear in mind what you identified in 'address the issues' regarding which benefits are most likely to appeal to your prospect.

Issue	Benefit that would most appeal

When, Where, How

Now think about the general method you would use when approaching this person:

- What time of day? Are they a morning person?
- What day? Is earlier in the week better or late Friday afternoon? When would they be most receptive?
- Would having a separate conversation just about your idea be better, or could you 'blend' it into a more general discussion?
- Bearing in mind the type of person they are (this is from what we looked at in 'understand the person' section), what persuasive words might work best? How will you manage the mood and tempo most appropriate to the person?
- What sort of response might they give to your idea? What concerns might they have? How will you answer those reactions with empathy?

Now, having done that, you need to consider the words you are going to use and how you would like to best phrase your presentation to suit the person and the situation. If you write down what you intend to say, it is worth remembering that words can have a different meaning when they are put on paper. However, the process of writing down what you plan to say may force you to think through the best options. We will go through three stages of preparing the best approach, as they are all to some extent different. All three are essential in helping us to find the best options and so achieve the best results:

- **Thinking it through**—we develop in our mind and thoughts what might be the best way to present an idea.

- **Writing it out**—when we are forced to 'unpack our thinking', we sift, sort and edit the words as they come out onto paper. Sometimes the words, when written, appear differently than your mind may have perceived.
- **Verbalising what is written**—we may find that some words or approaches do not sit well or feel appropriate. The act of reading it out will help give you another perspective that thinking it and writing it wouldn't identify so readily.

Furthermore, if you read the words out, you may again want to change and adapt, which can only be a good thing.

Using the template below, capture some thoughts as to how you might construct and 'couch' your idea by thinking of specific words and phrases you feel may be most appropriate. Then read it out loud. Almost certainly you'll want to change it, from what you had written down to the spoken word. Similarly, the first time you read your text aloud you may also feel the need to fine tune what you are going to say. This is a definite approach, but you should not be afraid to keep making changes until you think you have everything exactly right.

Ask yourself as you do this:

- What benefits am I offering?
- If I were that person, would I be influenced by what you are saying?
- How could you appeal to their interests more?
- Bearing in mind their personal style, would any other words or phrases 'push their buttons' even more?
- If someone was going to give you feedback on what you've written or said (now there's an idea!), what would it be? In what section?

Persuade—The Model

Worksheet template

Context	
Lead in	
Benefit	
Proposal	
Benefit	
Feedback	

In summary of this Deliver Benefits section of PERSUADE, it is impossible for you to do this as well as you could unless you have read and understood the earlier parts of PERSUADE, notably of course E (expand your understanding) and U (understand the person)

> **Quick activity**
>
> Think what the best outcome from the person you wish to persuade will be.
>
> In addition, think: What if they didn't agree to that? What might the second-best outcome be from your point of view? What else might they agree to that moves you both further down the road; albeit not as far as you'd first hoped.

So that leaves us with the final part of PERSUADE...

The P.E.R.S.U.A.D.E. model

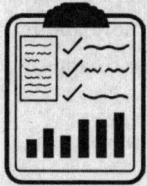

Evaluate the outcome

Aim

- To make sure the result is what you wanted to achieve

Being able to measure how successful you have been is important. It is entirely possible that the person you were persuading is someone you may well be in constant contact with, and there may be further opportunities when you need to convince that same person on a separate issue. By evaluating now, you can consider any changes you may wish to make to your approach and incorporate them into your conversation on the next occasion when you may seek to persuade that person.

When we evaluate, we make sure that our intention has had the desired effect. The obvious way to evaluate is to determine whether your prospect has taken the action you wanted them to.

- Have they understood your message and the thinking behind it?
- Have you achieved a common understanding? Check for understanding and mutual clarity.

My Persuasion objective	• For Julie to agree to and support the idea of Monday morning meetings
What steps I took	• I asked questions and found more about Julie's interests, so I knew how to appeal to her • I considered Julie's style when approaching her • I used appropriate benefits that would have the most appeal to Julie
What they did	• Listened to my ideas • Verbally supported the idea to the team and me over the next two weeks, when the matter came up increasingly for discussion (at my instigation) • Verbally and demonstrably supported the idea of a team get-together • Championed the idea and used some of the benefits she might get to one member of the team that wasn't sure at first
Difference	• None. I got more than I expected, and the result was more than I desired in the first place • I need to understand more about why this is so
Change next time	• Find out what it took for Julie to support and champion my idea in the way that she did • Do more of what it took!

Monday meetings were started some five weeks after I pitched the idea to Julie and today the meetings go from strength to strength. Since that time, I have had a conversation with Julie about something else, and the subject of the Monday meetings arose. This prompted me to ask Julie why she felt comfortable supporting the idea. She said:

> *"Well, I'll be honest with you that at first I was very against the idea because of some bad experiences I have had in the past. But I was astonished that I found myself coming around to the idea the more we talked.*
>
> *"I found that there were more reasons to support the idea you put forward. I found I was able to 'compartmentalise' my thoughts and experiences from the past and move on. The plan, as we talked it through, appealed increasingly and seemed to make sense all around; not just to me but with significant benefits for the team and the department.*
>
> *"So, I thought—let's go for it and put the idea forward. I'm with you."*

Now, I know that Julie, despite being fictitious, is a considerate person and will always investigate an opportunity when it is put to her. In the case of persuading her to become involved with the Monday meetings, she clearly saw the benefits to be gained by accepting this opportunity.

Of course, we can wonder whether she gave her support because that was part of her makeup or because I had considered how I would approach her using the P.E.R.S.U.A.D.E. model. What do you think?

SUMMARY

How does the use of the PERSUADE acronym help us?

We live in a world today where we are swamped with messages and communications that are being thrown at us to try to persuade us to buy every conceivable commodity or service. Strategies and tactics are becoming increasingly sophisticated and subtle.

I suppose, like all things, when it comes to making progress when searching for answers and ideas, we are encouraged to go **'back to basics'**. This is encapsulated best in Steven Coveys' masterful book *7 Habits of Highly Effective People*. Habit number five is *"Seek first to understand before you seek to be understood"*. Wise words!

What more elegant way to live up to Steven Covey's quotation can there be but to follow the PERSUADE model. With this model to assist you, you can plan and prepare more efficiently. Taking the model's lead will ensure that your insights into your prospect's style and temperament are considered. It will provide you with the insight to clarify some objective criteria and gain agreement from those you wish to persuade. The PERSUADE model will support your ideas and assumptions, and you can determine if they are valid by use of a summary. With that broad understanding, you can present your proposition to address the issues phrased in a manner best suited to the person you wish to persuade by highlighting values that are meaningful to them. The PERSUADE model also encourages you to evaluate the outcome of your approach by assessing whether you have achieved your objective, and, if not, what you should do next. Either way, there are likely to be many ways that you will discover that will help to improve your skills of persuasion for the next person and topic.

REFLECT AND LEARN

What ideas from this chapter were novel, fresh or new to you? What teaching was familiar? In what ways do you already apply some of what you have learned?

How did you react emotionally and cognitively to the ideas in this chapter? What concepts do you agree with and why? What do you disagree with and why?

What were the most exciting or useful insights gained from reading and thinking about this chapter?

In what ways might you translate the ideas presented in this chapter into practical, everyday, useful ideas and plans?

What new questions about persuasion do you now have after reading this chapter?

ACTION LEARNING

In addition to the original three examples you selected at the beginning of the book, make a list of other people and situations you could pass your learning experiences of persuasion to.

Set yourself some time-phased goals to apply some of what you have learned and listed in the Reflect and Learn section; some goals to guide your actions over the next three months, the next three weeks, and the next three days.

Thinking about how you plan to apply your learning, what obstacles might you encounter along the way? And, realistically, how might you deal with them?

Who else could you share these ideas with as a supportive sounding board or informal coach? How might you go about setting up a conversation with them to enrol them in supporting your application of this teaching? What might be some of the reasons why they would consider becoming involved? How might they also benefit?

4
Other Factors That Persuade

Persuasion can be a complex business that is not easily solved or achieved every time by using any one process or technique. This is because each person is different, every situation is different, and the human dynamics are always different. The skilled persuader is conscious of this and may use other methods at his/her disposal to help the persuasion process.

- People's emotions are powerful in the persuasion process—let's consider ways we can stimulate them
- Involving people in a variety of ways engages them and helps the persuasion process
- People believe others who they think are like themselves. How can this work for you?
- Being flexible and adaptable when persuading allows us to better understand the other person, communicate more effectively and persuade more successfully

Other factors to consider in the art of persuasion:

Third party reference

This is arguably the most effective form of marketing and if used correctly is highly persuasive. It is based on the old principle that "If you say it they doubt it—if someone else says it, it is true". We only need to look around us anywhere in the world today to see just how effectively this principle is being used in advertising or marketing to gain people's attention and to sway their thinking.

"Don't take our word for it..."

"78% of people asked said..."

"Eight out of ten pet owners agree that..."

Probably one of the most significant and most influential uses of third-party reference in recent times was "A million housewives every day, pick up a tin of beans and say, B-e-a-n-z M-e-a-n-z H-e-i-n-z".

Indeed, for retail consumers, it is a significant factor in the use of persuasion that may influence them to use or switch to another product. This element of third-party reference can very often override other vital factors that on other occasions would have a dominant effect on the buying decision. These include price, product quality and availability. I knew one person who was so influenced by what prominent people were saying about a product that it became almost the only factor. This product was far more expensive than she would usually pay, and the only place she could buy it was at Harrods in London, some 200 miles from where she lived!

- Have you ever been influenced to decide/buy something due to third-party reference?
- Have you ever used third-party reference in the past during the process of influencing someone?
- How could you use this concept currently with someone you would like to persuade?

Can it be used elsewhere? Businesses involved in the business-to-business process of selling do well by recognising the power of third-party reference. Indeed, the more 'switched-on' and 'savvy' business collects relevant and up-to-date testimonials as part of their approach to attracting new customers. These testimonial letters can be used with powerful effect to show how a similar business to the ones they are targeting has had a similar need satisfied in an exemplary way. The targeted business may well be reticent about being bowled over by the salesperson's patter, but is undeniably impressed, or 'persuaded', by a similar business with much the same needs that apparently has no personal stake in whether the business being targeted buys the seller's products or not.

Involvement

One of the most effective ways to get a genuine commitment from anyone is through involvement.

- **Why is involvement so effective?** By being involved, you become part of the scenario or situation put forward in some small way. Once you become involved with the 'problem' situation painted for you, it is only natural that you mentally, emotionally (and hopefully physically) will know a good solution when you see it and will feel involved enough to want to act on that.
- **How can I involve people?** There are many ways to involve people depending on the process and method by which you are persuading; whether it is face-to-face, in a letter or email, on the phone, etc. Among the ways are:
  a) Ask questions
  b) Use rhetorical questions
  c) Give them an analogy—ask them for an analogy
  d) Paint a picture with them in it—ask them to paint a picture
  e) Use stories—ask them for a relevant story

f) Ask for their opinion
g) Ask for their ideas/solutions—get them to write out a list
h) Make things relevant to them
i) Get them physically involved

Relevance

The more relevant a message is to you and your own set of circumstances, the more you feel you can connect with the meaning of it and the more you feel involved and likely to want to do something. When we looked at Ethos, Pathos, and Logos earlier in the book, we looked at how you can do more of this.

In simple terms, you should keep the 'wants' and 'needs' of the other person uppermost in your mind always and consider these when communicating information. Ask yourself: "How is this relevant to the other person?"

Keeping it relevant is your prospect's motivation for listening. The moment my communication becomes irrelevant then I must ask myself:
- "Why should they continue listening?"
- "Why should they show any interest, let alone act on what I am saying?"

Caring for me

I don't care how much you know until I know how much you care.

This fills one of our most profound human needs—to be cared for. The more I feel you care about me, my needs and wants through the focus of the communication and the questions you ask, the more significant my sense of empathy and gravitation will be towards you. I am likely to be more receptive, more open to ideas, more willing to listen to you and more willing to consider your thoughts.

The law of reciprocation suggests that if you care enough about me on the things that matter to me, then I will reciprocate by showing an interest in you and be more receptive to your communication.

The example given earlier in the section on Pathos is a clear example of the law of reciprocation. Remember the response of the man on the street when asked about something the US President had said on the news about the economy? The member of the public, in his piquant response, said: "I am not at all interested in what the President said and won't listen to him. After all, he never listens to us."

Fear of loss—desire to gain

These are the two most deep-seated motivators that are, in some ways, the root causes of why we do anything. You can take and consider anything you have chosen to do in your life, and after asking why you did it and what the motivators were, you will be able to come back to one or both factors.

Some people may go through their entire lives making decisions on the fear of loss. Their desire to do something is trying to avoid something. "I will do this, as I don't want this to happen."

What you must find out from the person you seek to persuade is which of these factors is the stronger for them in this case. Then, of course, you must determine through understanding what it is your prospect fears losing or desires to gain.

- Time?
- Respect?

- Credibility?
- Results?
- Efficiency?
- Control?

Conformity

This is like 'third-party reference' but in a more subtle way. It is part of the normal social pressures we all feel to conform to the society we live in. Conformity is a type of social influence involving a change in belief or behaviour to fit in with a specific group. This change is in response to real or imagined group pressure. There have been many experiments in psychology investigating conformity in connection with group pressure.

Robert Cialdini proposes the principle of social proof: "One means we use to determine what is correct is to find out what other people think is correct... We view a behaviour as more correct in each situation to the degree that we see others performing it. It operates most powerfully when we are observing the behaviour of people just like us." This, according to Cialdini, accounts for the preponderance of testimonials by 'ordinary' people on television. The tendency for people to 'follow suit' trades on that same bandwagon.

Psychologist Solomon Asch conducted a series of experiments during the 1950s designed to demonstrate the power of conformity in groups. In Asch's experiments, students were told that they were participating in a 'vision test'. Unbeknownst to the subjects, the other participants in the research were all confederates or assistants of the experimenter.

At first, the confederates answered the questions correctly but eventually began providing incorrect answers. Nearly 75% of the participants in the conformity experiments went along with the rest of the group at least once. After combining the trials, the results indicated that participants conformed to the incorrect group answer approximately one-third of the time. To ensure that participants were able to accurately gauge the length of the lines, they were asked to individually write down the correct match. According to these results, participants were very accurate in their line judgments, choosing the right answer 98% of the time.

After the experiments, participants were asked why they had gone along with the rest of the group. In most cases, the students stated that while they knew the rest of the group was wrong, they did not want to risk facing ridicule.

The Asch conformity experiments are among the most famous in psychology's history and have inspired a wealth of additional research on conformity and group behaviour. Jenness (1932) was the first psychologist to study conformity. His experiment was an ambiguous situation involving a glass bottle filled with beans. He asked participants individually to estimate how many beans the bottle contained. Jenness then put the group in a room with the bottle and asked them to provide a group estimate through discussion. Participants were then asked to estimate the number on their own again to find whether their initial forecast had altered based on the influence of the majority. Jenness then interviewed the participants individually again and asked if they would like to change their original estimates or stay with the group's assessment.

Interestingly, almost all changed their individual guesses to be closer to that of the group estimate. This can be linked to a student's experiment (see below) in March 2012, when participants were asked to estimate how much money was in a jar and to provide their own guess at the value. The aim of the experiment was very similar, only this time a different method was employed to support or disprove the hypothesis.

In a UK West Country university in March 2012, a psychology student undertook a similar experiment some 60 years after the Jenness experiment. Her investigation attempted to mislead participants when they were presented with an ambiguous situation. This would show conformity, as they would give their answers in a manner that took account of guesses made by other participants. The sample of participants was 20 people, a mixture of men and women and with an age range of 19 - 56. They were shown a jar of pennies and were asked to guess how much money was in it. They were randomly divided into two groups of ten. One group was shown a small table of fake, misleading answers; the other group had no access to the misleading information whatsoever. The result of this experiment demonstrated conformity, as the team that had been shown the misleading data gave, on average, much higher answers than the control group.

The main conclusion of all this research is that conformity does exist in situations where we may not expect it to. Even when information is written on paper, this can still affect us in our decision making. It would be fair to say that during the 1930s, people were encouraged to conform, whereas nowadays individualism is embraced far more—and yet those 2012 results show conformity is still working quite nicely thank you.

Deposits in the relationship bank account

Consciously or otherwise, we have an opinion about everyone. Our view will determine our subsequent behaviour and reactions towards them, and to any request they make of us. So, with everyone, there exists an 'emotional' or 'relationship' bank account to some degree. Some people are in credit with us emotionally, others are in debt. What is critical is that certainly, with the people we consider important in our lives, and the ones that we seek to persuade most frequently, we are 'in credit' with them with regards to the relationship bank account. The reason for this is that when we have a desire to persuade someone, we invariably wish to make a 'withdrawal' on that relationship bank account by asking them to do something or to agree with what we are suggesting.

Are you in credit with the people, or person, you wish to persuade?

With someone who is in credit, we will probably move heaven and earth to do what they ask of us. With someone who is in debt, where we have a choice, we are more inclined to say 'no' to someone who is severely overdrawn, often by inwardly groaning, when their name appears on our phone, and we switch the call off.

Generally, in any relationship, the interactions and behaviours that are exchanged are when we are depositing or withdrawing from the emotional bank. Like any bank balance, when an account is overdrawn, the easiest way to rectify the situation is to inject a few credits into the account. And, like a real bank account, there is an exchange rate mechanism! Remaining in credit is essential to your credibility and your ability to persuade more effectively.

The thing to stay mindful of is that we are always happy to make withdrawals—favours, ask for time, help and support, but do we readily and proactively make deposits in the same, or a greater, proportion?

> **Factors that could act as credits**
> - Listen to me
> - Give me time
> - Say thank you to me
> - Always being there for me
> - Show you value me
> - Gives me specific positive feedback
> - Do something I appreciate when I have not asked
> - Do things for me when YOU don't want anything back

Why would someone making deposits to the relationship bank account to keep it in credit help? Because we feel a strong kinship with a person who has made deposits, so store such acts in our memory either consciously or subconsciously. When it comes to persuading that person, even without reminding them of our past actions, they will often be aware of the credits in our account with them or they may, in a non-conscious way, simply feel predisposed towards us. Although on its own it won't be enough merely to persuade, they certainly will help keep rapport in place and may well fuel their propensity to want to do something for you.

Push their 'hot' buttons

'Hot' buttons are points, topics or subjects that stir up a range of emotions within someone. This feeling may be anger, joy, excitement, passion, enthusiasm or desire. Hot buttons commonly surface through general day-to-day dialogue when one person suddenly reacts in a more animated way than usual when a specific topic is discussed. They may say such things as:

> *"Don't get me started on traffic wardens..."*
> *"That is one of my pet hates..."*
> *"This is something I feel really strongly about..."*

Hot buttons can be called 'hot' because someone feels strongly or passionately about something. Depending on what you are trying to influence someone about, if the hot button that you press concerns a subject they are not averse to, then it could work in your favour.

Of course, you can only use hot buttons to your advantage once they are known to you, and you proactively aim to push the button at an opportune time. So, how can you approach this?

Find a topic that appears to be a hot button—The first thing to do is to get to know as much as you can about the person you wish to influence by investing time. Asking questions to understand the person's desires, needs and motives will eventually give you enough information to allow you the opportunity to identify with their hot buttons.

Of course, it may well be that you don't know the person you are aiming to persuade very well, but someone else has warned you not to broach a subject that may cause animosity or displeasure. Conversely, a third party may also advise you of which matters to approach to obtain a positive response.

> *"Don't get him started on..."*
> *"Get onto the subject of tennis with him, and he'll talk for hours. You'll be his best friend...!"*

Hot buttons are useful to know because they evoke strong feelings that can lead to the other person voicing firm opinions or making instant decisions. Such decisions could be used to readily influence their actions, particularly if they can undoubtedly be 'hung' on their strong feelings about a subject.

Affirm it—Hearsay is one thing but finding out for yourself is another. It is better to have your own evidence and to be able to affirm for yourself that a topic can trigger a hot button. If you intend using an area or theme that you suspect is a hot button that you have gained from another source, ask a tentative probing question, or make a statement about that subject to stimulate a reaction.

Push it—Push it merely means that you deliberately ask a question or make a comment about a known hot button that aims to get the other person enthused when you talk about their favourite subject.

Of course, you must pick the most appropriate moment to do this and be sure you know what you want to do with the reaction once you get it. It is best to be able to connect the hot-button topic in some way with the response you are likely to get, and then guide the other person towards the area of influence you wish to follow.

The contrast principle

The contrast principle says that when you experience two similar things in quick succession, your perception of the second is influenced by the first. We tend to non-consciously notice the difference in characteristics rather than absolute measures.

We judge pretty much anything in comparison with something else. When we say someone is smart or talkative, we are saying the individual is smarter or more verbose than other people we know.

Put your left hand in a bowl of cold water and your right in hot water. Leave them there for a while, then plunge both hands together into a bowl of lukewarm water. Try it, and your left hand will feel hot while the right hand will feel cold.

If you pick up a heavy box first and then immediately pick up a light one, the second one will feel lighter than it really is. This is how our perceptions are shaped and influenced by what goes on around us, and it happens in ways we are generally not aware of.

Similarly, once you have already agreed to something large, additional items that are added seem smaller by comparison. Sales professionals use this technique to sell options and accessories to large ticket items people have already agreed to buy.

So, what? Contrast is an important principle by which we make decisions, so to persuade someone using this principle we get them to pay attention to one or more comparisons.

If we quoted someone an item with a high price first, and then a lower priced one shortly after, the second would seem lower to that person than it really is, and they are likely to consider it more favourably.

If you show someone a lower quality product alongside the one that you want your prospect to buy, especially if they are challenging its price, you might also show them a fantastic product that is way beyond their reach. When they compare their ideal purchase with this higher value option, they are then likely to re-evaluate upwards.

The key is controlling the comparator. Once you have identified the decisions that you want the other person to make, identify the comparator that they are likely to use naturally and then work to replace it with your preferred comparator.

It is possible to stretch their range of options by making it better or worse than they were expecting. You can also change their priorities, for instance by using quality or availability instead of cost.

Telling a story they can immerse themselves in

Over 60% of people today have a strong visual preference for how they reference information and make sense of it. This means that they prefer to see things as visual communication, so they can make sense of it, rather than rely purely on the spoken word.

Imagine how a non-visual person may try to influence someone who is extremely visual. How will someone that is less visual achieve this? The likelihood is that they will talk things through and explain their idea and what they want the other person to do. How successful are they likely to be? Not very.

The other person is unlikely to make any sense of the information although it may be conveyed in clear spoken English (or their native tongue). But, if there is minimal visual stimulus coming their way, they may struggle to make sense of the information. We all know of people who have communicated something that is seemingly quite clear to them, yet the other person has a blank expression and asks, "Can you go through it again—I don't get it." An exchange of this kind is not at all uncommon.

I recall one occasion where the person who was trying to be persuaded was very visual, yet the communication he was being subjected to was conducted purely verbally. The person trying to explain his ideas offered no visual stimulus at all. Yet the recipient was so desperate for something to reference the message visually that after listening, he picked up a piece of paper and drew a flowchart with a series of steps, then showed it to the person delivering the message and said, "Is this what you mean?"

Of course, the person who was trying to persuade him looked somewhat quizzical and said, "Yes, of course," thinking to himself 'Isn't that just what I have been saying?'

What's the message here?

When influencing, it pays to make sure that there are things that will 'stimulate' the visual elements in a person's thinking. Of course, there are many things people do to achieve this including showing images, pictures, PowerPoint presentations, photos, graphs, hand-outs plus many others.

However, telling a story that they can relate to, and that they can immerse themselves in, works particularly well. Why? Because you have caught their attention and imagination and have been 'part of the scenario' from the beginning. Because both parties are involved, it makes any form of disassociation difficult. Decision making and commitment between the person doing the persuading and the recipient, therefore, is far easier. A simple rule to follow with storytelling is: 'no involvement, no commitment' and vice-versa.

Remember too that the story must have a point and must be relevant to the issues upon which you are trying to influence and engage your prospect. When you get to the point in your story you are intent on making, the prospect will not only see it more plainly but will also understand the value of your idea.

Here are three ways to help immerse someone visually:

Real life situation—relating or recounting a real story of something that happened either to you or someone else, if the scenario is one that they can relate to because they have been in a similar situation or could have been!

"Let me share an experience with you that my business had five years ago. On this specific day, all seemed normal as it is now..."

Paint a picture of an imaginary situation—Imagine you are walking down a country lane late at night. It is cold, and you can see your breath in front of you in the crisp night air.

You can see the stars very clearly. As you look at them, you think, "There are SO many".

Analogy—offering your prospect a scenario that they may be familiar with often relates well. "Analogies prove nothing that is true," wrote Sigmund Freud, "but they can make one feel more at home."

Consider a couple of analogies here:

Analogy one

"The great Argentine footballer, Diego Maradona, is not usually associated with the theory of monetary policy," Mervyn King explained to an audience in the City of London a few years ago, "but the player's performance for Argentina against England in the 1986 World Cup perfectly summarised modern central banking," the Bank of England's sport-loving governor added.

"Maradona's infamous 'hand of God' goal, which should have been disallowed, reflected old-fashioned central banking, Mr King said. It was full of mystique and "he was lucky to get away with it". But the second goal, where Maradona beat five players before scoring, even though he ran in a straight line, was an example of modern practice. "How can you beat five players by running in a straight line? The answer is that the English defenders reacted to what they expected Maradona to do. Monetary policy works in a similar way. Market interest rates react to what the central bank is expected to do." (Chris Giles, "Alone Among Governors", Financial Times. Sep. 8-9, 2007)

Analogy two

"Pupils are more like oysters than sausages. The job of teaching is not to stuff them and then seal them up, but to help them open

and reveal the riches within. There are pearls in each of us, if only we knew how to cultivate them with ardour and persistence." (Sydney J. Harris, "What True Education Should Do", 1964)

Although not quite an analogy (more possibly a metaphor), I remember selling classified advertising for the *Daily Mail* many years ago and one of the selling points was the fact that in a specific category of the readership we had over 94,000 readers with the desired profile. However, to communicate the position more strongly, I used the analogy of Wembley Stadium being full of the type of people the potential advertiser wished to target. The image of Wembley full of people they wanted had more power than just the figures.

Embedded commands

Here is a potent tool of influence, one that can transform your ability to create conviction and belief in others. Used correctly, you will have the opportunity to turn a mere presentation into a dynamic opportunity to secure committed action. This tool will make you a robust, efficient and more prosperous influencer. The opportunities this will present to you are truly immense.

This tool, known as 'chunks of belief' (or embedded commands), is based on an understanding of human psychology and motivation. It addresses people's needs to be moved emotionally and convinced intellectually. It is used in different forms by hypnotists, advertisers and even novelists such as Tom Clancy! It produces belief and conviction instead of merely interest.

When I first learned this tool, I was amazed how well it worked with everyone I encountered. I even used it to convince my then 11-year-old daughter (she's a little older now) to enjoy her drama lessons. It also works in writing and mail-shots.

Isn't that something worth taking some time to understand?

If you thought 'Yes' to the last question, then you have experienced a chunk of belief in action as an embedded command.

A piece of belief as an embedded command is delivered in a sequence of steps:

1. State a big claim (first sentence)
2. Tell people what it will mean to them in general terms (second sentence)
3. Make a more personal benefits statement (third and fourth sentences)
4. Give logical evidence (like the second paragraph)
5. Give emotional or story-based proof (like the third paragraph)
6. Ask for action, or try a test close

So how does it work?

State a big claim—Now we are going to examine a potent tool of influence, one that can transform your ability to create conviction and belief in others.

Tell people what it will mean to them in general terms—Appropriately used, you will have the opportunity to turn a mere presentation into a dynamic opportunity to secure committed action.

Make a more personal benefits statement—This tool will make you a powerful, effective and more successful influencer. The opportunities that this will open to you are truly immense.

Give relevant evidence—This tool, known as 'chunks of

belief', is based on an understanding of human psychology and motivation. It produces belief and conviction instead of merely interest.

Give emotional or story-based evidence—When I first learned this tool I was amazed how well it worked with everyone I encountered. It also works in writing and mailshots.

Ask for action or a test close—Isn't that something worth taking some time to understand?

Using this sequence, what happens?

Firstly, we get attention with our big claim. It won't be believed, but that's not the point. The only aim is to get someone's attention.

Then, we start to engage their emotions and desire with a benefit statement that is quite general. This also gets the imagination going. We then accelerate the process by making the benefits much more personal and meaningful to them. Of course, if we are face-to-face, this can be more targeted than in a mailshot, or even as an email!

The logical evidence (statistics, theory, research, etc) starts to prove that your claim is valid and that the desire can be fulfilled. The emotional testimony (stories, metaphors, examples, quotes, etc) then complete the cycle by giving even more evidence that the passion you have created can be met. Some people will respond better to the logical, others to the emotional, but everyone will be touched by one or the other, and most people by both. Your call to action or test close (by merely asking someone if they think that what you have said to this point is a good idea) then produces commitment.

So, now that you understand all of this, you might be willing to try it. I suggest trying it in writing first, where the structure is more precise, and then working your way up to putting the whole thing together into a conversation.

Of course, once you have put some work into this, you can stack chunks of belief, so that you can embed small pieces inside bigger ones.

Persuasive words

The choice of words is important as they create positive or negative images. Choose words which develop positive models to trigger the right emotional response. Some words can irritate, for example: 'with all due respect' or 'let's be realistic' can be perceived as patronising or aggressive.

Avoid jargon which may confuse your listener. Instead, empathise with them. Ensure your vocabulary is broad enough, enabling you to express your ideas and feelings in ways which demonstrate that you do understand the thoughts and beliefs of your listener.

Negative words	<ul><li>Perhaps</li><li>Possibly</li><li>Maybe</li><li>Can't</li><li>Problem</li><li>Difficulty</li></ul>
Positive words	<ul><li>Certainly</li><li>Immediately</li><li>Of course</li><li>Solution</li><li>Opportunity</li></ul>

Persuasive words	<ul><li>Success</li><li>Results</li><li>Improve</li><li>Gain</li><li>Enhance</li><li>Benefit</li></ul>

Words should be simple and easy to understand and help the listener to appreciate precisely what you mean, and tap straight into their thought process. The persuasive words are designed to help and support your listener to make the 'right' decision.

Use Positive Language

In general, when trying to convince someone, always talk about positive things and pleasant memories, never the bad things that happened. We tend to gravitate and relate most to success stories. Equally importantly, we gravitate to positive people. We feel good about ourselves by being in the company of positive people and are possibly more amenable to suggestion consequently. Talk about positive experiences, positive outcomes and positive results.

Positive people in the world are regarded as 'radiators', and negative people are viewed as 'vacuum cleaners' or 'drains'. Positive people are perceived to 'radiate' positive energy, thoughts and feelings. They create a climate and mood of positivity of hope, opportunity and possibility and as such, encourage and familiarise thought processes along those lines.

People who use negative words, phrases, examples and stories are generally perceived as 'vacuum cleaners' because they suck up all the natural energy in a room. Someone once said that a vacuum cleaner can brighten up a room immediately merely by leaving it.

People like to linger and look and spend lots of time with, and be associated with, people who radiate energy, while most people tend to move away from a vacuum cleaner after a few minutes.

Just imagine, if you were walking down the street and you saw a well-known 'vacuum cleaner' walking toward you, what would you do? That's right—you would do almost anything to avoid that person because of the way they make you feel. In fact, you'd probably cross the street just to avoid them.

Remember though, that if you are walking down the street and you see a 'radiator' coming toward you, start worrying when you look and see that person crossing the street!

Reverse psychology/Scarcity

The key here with both these points is that a perceived limitation of something will generate demand.

Reverse psychology

Reverse psychology is when you tell someone to do the opposite of what you want them to do. German psychologists Theodor Adorno (1903–1969) and Max Horkheimer (1895–1973) theorised that people respond in an opposite or reverse direction of what they are told, and this theory has been tested and proved many times since the idea's rise to prominence in the 1970s' fitness and jogging boom.

I am sure, dear reader, we have all at one point or another in our lives offered, or made available, something to our friends or family, only to withdraw it in jest at some point later. After someone flounders on deciding whether they want something, you then take it away with: "No, you can't have it now", only to find that they now DO want it and probably yearn for it more. A great example can be taken from an episode of *The Simpsons* cartoon TV series where Homer is busy talking to himself.

Homer's Brain: *"Don't you get it? You've got to use reverse psychology."*
Homer: *"That sounds too complicated."*
Homer's Brain: *"OK, don't use reverse psychology."*
Homer: *"All right, I will!"*

I remember how one salesperson used reverse psychology on a prospective client by saying:

> *"With a lot of our clients like yourselves, they benefited by having this particular service. However, we didn't feel that would appeal to you so haven't put it forward in our proposal."*

Sure enough, the client got particularly interested, thinking: 'Why wouldn't I want these benefits?' The salesman figured that if the buyer DIDN'T want it, then it supported his point and that his thought process and intention was right for the client. However, he was familiar with the concept of reverse psychology and knew that many prospects want to look for evidence of the opposite of what a salesperson is suggesting.

Scarcity

"Whatever is rare, uncommon or dwindling in availability—this idea of scarcity—confers value on objects or even relationships", says Robert Cialdini, Regents' Professor of Psychology and Marketing at Arizona State University and Distinguished Professor of Marketing in the W. P. Carey School.

A lady rings her local computer store: "Have you any of those laptops left with an XYZ processor?"

The man at the computer shop standing next to a massive pile of laptops with XYZ processor: "Mmm, let me see. Hang on a minute." (Shouts away from the mouthpiece) "Jim, have we got any of those laptops left with an XYZ processor?"

Jim's muffled voice in the background: "Yes, I think we have just one left."

The man goes back on the phone to the lady prospect: "Yes, I think we have one left."

Lady prospect: "Oh good. Can you put my name on it and put it aside for me please?"

The scarcity, of course, could be time, money, data, knowledge, and any other number of things.

With regards to time, one freelance marketing consultant in Paris regularly uses scarcity to help 'persuade' prospects to use her services. When clients approach the area of timescales and availability she always says:

> "I want to find you the best option here so can you give me three minutes?"

She then goes on to ask if she can call them back in three minutes. Those three minutes, of course, are intriguing, as most people would ask for either two minutes or five minutes. So, part of the prospect's brain has an internal dialogue: "Why three minutes?"

Checking she has the right number and the fact that the prospect will indeed be there in three minutes, the marketing consultant calls back and suggests she can only offer one, or maybe two blocks of time to work on their project (she needed the three minutes to see if she could reorganise specific prior arrangements). Invariably she reports that the perception of scarcity she has created encourages the prospective client not only to decide on one of the two options but to want to do that there and then.

Have we all succumbed to scarcity at some point or other?

Emotions

Some years ago, Harvard University conducted a study about the factors that drive a buying decision, and they found that 84% of any decision is made from an emotional base and 16% from a logical base. In more recent years, various scientific tests have concluded that emotions often get overlooked, yet are a significant factor in how people make decisions. Emotions are very often the things that override logic. I am sure we have all done it: we have looked in a shop window at a suit, a shirt, a dress, blouse, etc, and admired it. We know in our mind that there are logical reasons not to buy it:

1. I have enough of this type of garment at home
2. I can't afford it, I have very little money

Yet, as you and I know, we may very often come away with what we saw because we admired it and saw ourselves in it. It evoked some strong emotions that may well be connected to image, confidence and choice. Of course, this is true with so many of the daily decisions we make, whether it is to buy a bigger house or whether to submit to someone's request. Although such a request may be perfectly reasonable and achievable, not everyone will say 'yes'. This is because there may be stronger forces at work that are linked to the relationship, or indeed, our experiences of that relationship. All of which are emotional reasons.

Factors that can often affect emotions are:

- Hope
- Fear

- Excitement
- Frustration
- Enthusiasm
- Curiosity
- Passion
- Love
- Anger
- Security
- Love
- Care

So, if you are aiming to persuade someone, how could you use emotions to help you in your cause?

Stimulate an emotion—maybe there isn't a 'known' emotion (something that you know is a 'hot' button) that is a critical factor for the person you are aiming to influence. However, you can consider your idea and how it might stimulate one of the two primary emotional drivers connected to influencing:

1. Fear of loss of something
2. Desire for gain

If you can show that buying into your idea will help them **gain** something that you perceive could be of value to them, then you will engage them quicker. This could be represented by any number of gains that would benefit the prospect, such as:

- More time
- More control
- More peace of mind
- Greater credibility with others
- More success
- More productivity
- More confidence

If, however, you feel that stimulating a **fear of loss** would be useful, then you may be considering things such as:

- Missed opportunity
- Losing the competitive edge
- Lose sales, income or money
- Lose customers
- Be less effective

'Prick' an emotion—it may be that you know a specific form of emotion strikes a durable cord with the person you are persuading. For example, you may understand that he/she will always veer to making any decision that makes him/her feel comfortable. To them, it is all about security and peace of mind.

Or, perhaps you have a real appreciation from your past experiences with this person that they always like to strike out and take risks. If you presented them with a challenge, you know they invariably go for the option that carries some risk but potentially higher rewards whatever shape that may be.

Knowing what drives your prospect and motivates them will help you 'frame and position' your thoughts, ideas and proposals so that it 'pricks' that specific emotion and gives them the chance to take that risk or make that safe decision. By doing so, you know you will either stimulate or prick an emotive chord that can be far stronger than any logic you may choose to use.

Reciprocation

The law of reciprocation states that when someone does something for us, we feel compelled to return the favour. According to Robert B. Cialdini, author of *The Psychology of Persuasion*, the rule for reciprocation is:

> *"One of the most potent of the weapons of influence around us is the rule for reciprocation. The rule says that we should try to repay, in kind, what another person has provided us."*

So, if you want someone to do something good for you, why not do something good for them first? In a business setting, this might mean passing your prospect a lead. Maybe you can give them some useful market knowledge/intelligence that would help them?

In a domestic situation, you might offer to lend your lawnmower to a neighbour. It doesn't matter where or when you do it, the key is to complement the relationship.

'Yes' questions

This is called conditioning and is about getting the brain familiar with a specific pattern of answering. For example: ask somebody to answer three simple questions.

Question: "What noise does a frog make?" (Let them answer)

Answer: Croak

Question: "What is the name of a funny short story? (Let them answer)

Answer: A joke

Question: "What do you call the white of an egg?" (Let them answer)

Answer: Albumen (although invariably most people will say 'the yolk')

Why would they do that? Because their brain has become used to answering in a certain way with 'croak', 'joke' and, in line with the response, they think you are looking for 'yolk' as the third answer. So, you will notice from this that we don't fully listen to the question. Otherwise, we wouldn't say "yolk"! What we tend to do is to say what we *think* falls in line with the 'right answer'.

Similar examples are:

- Asking someone to spell 'mop', 'stop', 'crop' and 'drop'. What do you do when you come to a green traffic light? Without thinking, many people are likely to answer "stop" when they actually mean 'go'.
- Ask someone to the spell 'roast', 'coast', 'boast' and 'most', and then ask: "What do you put in the toaster?" Most will reply: "toast", when, of course, the correct answer is 'bread'.
- Ask someone to quickly repeat the word 'silk' ten times. After they do it, then ask them: "What do cows drink?" You've guessed it … they will probably answer "milk" when it's more likely (although I am not a farmer!) for cows to drink water.

So, how might this help when persuading someone? By doing this, it is possible to convince others in such a way that it can help encourage their brain pattern thinking in a certain way that would suit what we want to persuade them about.

Begin the conversation with questions that generate a "yes" response.

- "Nice day today, isn't it?"
- "You'd like to be clear how this can help you, right?
- "You're looking for a great deal on a car, aren't you?"

Once you get someone to say "yes", it's easier to get them to continue, up to and including "Yes, I'll buy it."

SUMMARY

We said in the introduction to this chapter that persuasion can be a complicated business. While the PERSUADE model offers you a stable process to plan and apply your communication, influencing and persuasive skills, this chapter provides you with insights into several other essential principles and techniques. The more you know about each of these useful ideas, the more efficient you are likely to be at persuading others. This is because every person is unique and will require almost a one-off approach explicitly designed for them.

We've covered several central topics such as:

- The use of third-party references to provide added credibility
- The method of involvement because even those solutions we have only partially added to and shape are hard not to see as our own
- Persuasive words, hot buttons and embedded commands
- Reverse Psychology
- Relationship bank accounts

We've also investigated the core of human motivation surrounding:

- Relevancy
- Conformity
- The fear of loss versus the desire for gain

Persuasion can be a complicated business that is not easily solved or achieved using a simple process or technique. This is because each person is different, each situation is different, and the human dynamics are always different. The skilled persuader is conscious of this and may use other methods at his/her disposal to assist the persuasion process, using story-telling blended with powerful words and embedded commands focussed on stimulating their hot buttons in a way that adds to our relationship bank account and is likely to be a hard approach to reject.

By understanding this range of tools, you can become more flexible and increasingly adaptable when approaching others to persuade them in an ethical, enhancing and efficient way.

REFLECT AND LEARN

What ideas from this chapter were novel, fresh or new to you? What learning was familiar? In what ways do you already apply some of this teaching?

How did you react emotionally and cognitively to the ideas in this chapter? What concepts do you agree with and why? What do you disagree with and why?

What were the most exciting or useful insights gained from reading and thinking about this chapter?

In what ways might you translate the ideas presented through this chapter into practice using common useful ideas and plans?

What new questions about persuasion do you now have after reading this chapter?

ACTION LEARNING

In addition to the original three examples you selected at the beginning of the book, list several other people and situations that could benefit from applying your learning on persuasion.

Set yourself some time-phased goals to apply some of the learning that you listed in the Reflect and Learn section, some goals to guide your actions over the next three months, the next three weeks and the next three days.

Thinking about how you plan to apply your learning and what obstacles you might encounter along the way, how might you deal with them realistically?

Who else could you share these ideas with as a supportive sounding board or informal coach? How might you go about setting up a conversation with them to enrol them in supporting your application of this teaching? What might be some of your reasons for believing they would consider being involved? How might they also benefit?

5

Famous and Infamous Stories of Persuasion

INTRODUCTION

Successful persuasion has been evident since almost the beginning of time. The great and the good over many years have offered us some fine examples of their own attempts at persuasion. Some of the following examples are dramatic and moving; some have been achieved very quickly; others took many, many years.

As we stated at the beginning of the book, we all have a need to persuade at some point or other in our lives. Let us reflect and enjoy some examples of famous and infamous past acts of persuasion. What lessons may we take from these?

- With an unswerving passion, persuasion can take place against seemingly insurmountable odds
- Being extraordinarily creative has a strong persuasive element
- What might appear as the easiest matter of persuasion can fall flat
- Having a strong emotional appeal can sometimes be successfully deployed to persuade even in the most difficult situations

The Queen—Who would have thought it?

In the opening ceremony of the London Olympics 2012, Her Majesty the Queen was persuaded to appear alongside Daniel 'James Bond 007' Craig to accompany him on a special mission. The Queen—who would have thought it?

Not since the young royals, Prince Edward and Sarah Ferguson, the former wife of Prince Andrew, appeared on the TV show *It's a Knockout* has ground been broken against perceived protocol, bringing the royals closer to the British public than ever before.

Apparently, even the Queen couldn't resist this invitation to star in the most talked-about sequence from organiser Danny Boyle. Fifty years ago such a request would probably have had you sent straight to the Tower! To be able to persuade the monarch to accept such a call at that time would have been a miracle.

But, accept she did. Her Majesty was persuaded, on one condition, more of which in a minute.

It all came about when Danny Boyle's idea was raised with London 2012 chief, Sebastian Coe.

Such an idea was thought impossible, the *Daily Mail* revealed, without the input of one man, a former adviser to William Hague, none other than the Queen's deputy private secretary, Edward Young. He acted as the liaison between Boyle's team and Buckingham Palace, which led some insiders to refer to Young as the 'Secret Agent'.

Lord Coe had served as chief of staff to William Hague around the time Young was working as the (then) opposition leader's communications chief, before taking up his role at Buckingham Palace in 2007. Such a connection gave the plan every chance of success.

So, what was the condition Her Majesty stipulated?

Apparently, her sole stipulation before taking up her acting role was that she would choose what to wear! She finally decided on a salmon-coloured dress, and not a royal equivalent of Wonder Woman as some might have preferred! After greeting Daniel Craig in rooms at Buckingham Palace, and following him down the corridors, she appears next parachuting from a helicopter into the Olympic Stadium.

In these scenes, doubles (naturally!) were used, notably Julia McKenzie, famed for portraying Miss Marple, playing the role of The Queen. The scene concluded with the stunt double of the Queen, daredevil Gary Connery, exiting the helicopter and parachuting into the Olympic Stadium.

Seconds later, the actual Queen, wearing the same dress as she did in the filmed sequence, was greeted with roars of laughter and a standing ovation as she entered the arena with Prince Philip.

So, what was it that persuaded the Queen to accept this most unusual invitation? Perhaps we'll never know, but it seems clear that what may not result in somebody being influenced one day, might turn into the opposite on a different day once the science of persuasion has done its work.

- If the scenario is deemed sufficiently attractive to the other person, the impossible may become possible
- Having good contacts and relationships can help 'oil' the persuasion process
- Being bold and adventurous when persuading can be acceptable if the context and situation allows it

The *Argument* sketch

Successful persuasion relies on individual elements being brought into play. Here are some of the required features of persuasion:

- A well-thought-out proposal paying particular attention to the known or perceived importance of the points raised about the other person that you are trying to influence
- Considerate positioning with the listener's interests and motivations in mind
- Asking insightful questions to encourage the other person to explore
- Playback and summary with repeating your understanding to demonstrate your awareness, or the pursuit thereof
- Empathy and support towards the views of the person you are trying to persuade
- Acceptance of disagreement with supporting behaviours and a line of reasoning
- Positioning your point of view so that it offers clear benefits to the other person
- Connecting with the person on a personal level, possibly through pace, tone and body language
- Playing to the relative importance of the other person

A stand-out example that demonstrates the opposite of what influencing *should* be is portrayed in the famous *Argument* sketch from *Monty Python's Flying Circus*. Written by John Cleese and Graham Chapman, this sketch was initially broadcast in 1972 and appeared in one of Monty Python's early long-playing vinyl records from the same period and was subsequently performed at their *Live at Drury Lane* show.

The entire basis of the sketch focuses on someone wanting to have an argument (as the title suggests!) as opposed to any form of influencing. The following is the script from the Monty Python sketch.

A man goes into room 12A. Another man is sitting behind a desk.

Man: Is this the right room for an argument?
Other Man: (pause) I've told you once.
Man: No, you haven't!
Other Man: Yes, I have.
M: When?
O: Just now.
M: No, you didn't!
O: Yes, I did!
M: You didn't!
O: I did!
M: You didn't!
O: I'm telling you, I did!
M: You didn't!
O: Oh, I'm sorry, is this a five-minute argument, or the full half hour?
M: Ah! (Taking out his wallet and paying) Just the five minutes.
O: Just the five minutes. Thank you.
O: Anyway, I did.
M: You most certainly did not!
O: Now let's get one thing entirely clear: I most definitely told you!
M: Oh no you didn't!
O: Oh yes, I did!
M: Oh no you didn't!
O: Oh yes, I did!
M: Oh no you didn't!
O: Oh yes, I did!
M: Oh no you didn't!
O: Oh yes, I did!

M: Oh no you didn't!
O: Oh yes, I did!
M: Oh no you didn't!
O: Oh yes, I did!
M: No, you DIDN'T!
O: Oh yes, I did!
M: No, you DIDN'T!
O: Oh yes, I did!
M: No, you DIDN'T!
O: Oh yes, I did!
M: Oh look, this isn't an argument!

(Pause)

O: Yes, it is!
M: No, it isn't!

(Pause)

M: It's just contradiction!
O: No, it isn't!
M: It IS!
O: It is NOT!
M: You just contradicted me!
O: No, I didn't!
M: You DID!
O: No no no!
M: You did just then!
O: Nonsense!
M: (exasperated) Oh, this is futile!!

(Pause)

O: No, it isn't!
M: Yes, it is!

(Pause)

M: I came here for a good argument!
O: AH, no you didn't, you came here for an argument!
M: An argument isn't just contradiction.
O: Well! It CAN be!
M: No, it can't!
M: An argument is a connected series of statements intended to establish a proposition.
O: No, it isn't!
M: Yes, it is! It isn't just contradiction?
O: Look, if I *argue* with you, I must take up a contrary position!
M: Yes, but it isn't just saying "no it isn't".
O: Yes, it is!
M: No, it isn't!
O: Yes, it is!
M: No, it isn't!
O: Yes, it is!
M: No, it ISN'T! Argument is an intellectual process. Contradiction is just the automatic gainsaying of anything the other person says.
O: It is NOT!
M: It is!
O: Not at all!
M: It is!

The Arguer hits a bell on his desk and stops.

O: Thank you, that's it.
M: (stunned) What?
O: That's it. Good morning.
M: But I was just getting interested!

O: I'm sorry, the five minutes is up.
M: That was never five minutes!!
O: I'm afraid it was.
M: (leading on) No it wasn't...
O: I'm sorry, I'm not allowed to argue anymore.
M: WHAT??
O: If you want me to go on arguing, you'll have to pay for another five minutes.
M: But that was never five minutes just now!
       Oh, come on!
       Oh, this is...
       This is ridiculous!
O: I told you...
       I told you, I'm not allowed to argue unless you PAY!
M: Oh, all right. (Takes out his wallet and pays again.) There you are.
O: Thank you.
M: (clears throat) Well...
O: Well WHAT?
M: That was never five minutes just now.
O: I told you, I'm not allowed to argue unless you've paid!
M: Well I just paid!
O: No, you didn't!
M: I DID!!!
O: YOU didn't!
M: I DID!!!
O: YOU didn't!
M: I DID!!!
O: YOU didn't!
M: I DID!!!
O: YOU didn't!
M: I don't want to argue about it!

O: Well I'm very sorry, but you didn't pay!
M: Ah Hah! Well if I didn't pay, why are you arguing??? Ah HAAAAAAHHH! Gotcha!
O: No, you haven't!
M: Yes, I have!
        If you're arguing, I must have paid.
O: Not necessarily.
        I *could* be arguing in my spare time.
M: I've had enough of this!
O: No, you haven't.

(Door slam)

For us to fully appreciate what influencing is, the script depicts the absence of any of the essential elements in the '*Argument*' sketch. Instead, it is the essence of being the complete opposite of influencing. Why?

The *Argument* sketch shows people who are:

- Self-centred
- Not 'asking' questions
- Dismissing each other's point of view

Simply put, you will never persuade someone if you become engaged in an argument.

The man who turned down The Beatles

One of the most famous history-in-the-making examples relating to persuasion was when Dick Rowe of Decca Records was the Artists and Repertoire (A&R) Executive. Mr Rowe became famous as the 'man who turned down the Beatles'.

In hindsight, it seems almost incredible that what might now seem to be the most straightforward and most effective action in the entire world failed to persuade the decision maker who could have given the Fab Four their big break and debut record deal.

Ironically, George Harrison later persuaded Dick Rowe to sign another up-and-coming group called The Rolling Stones to Decca Records, Rowe missed what can only be described as a 'golden opportunity' to sign the Beatles. This must have been a decision that haunted him right up until his death in June 1986.

The Beatles' famous audition for Decca Records took place in London on New Year's Day 1962.

The session followed the attendance of another of the label's A&R representatives, Mike Smith, at a Cavern Club performance on 13 December 1961. The Beatles' performance that night hadn't been strong enough to secure them a record deal, but the label was willing to offer them a session at its London studios. The group had an arduous journey to London in bad weather, and they arrived with little time to spare before the 11.00am start.

Things didn't go well, and the group was annoyed that Smith turned up late due to his New Year celebration the previous night. "I was pretty annoyed," Brian Epstein, The Beatles' manager, later recalled. "Not because we were anxious to tape our songs, but because we felt we were being treated as people who didn't matter." The Beatles were also expected to use Decca's equipment because the record company believed that the group's own, which they had brought with them, wasn't good enough. "They didn't want our tackle," recalled Neil Aspinall, the Beatles' roadie. "We had to use theirs. We needn't have dragged our amps all the way from Liverpool."

The Beatles recorded 15 songs altogether. Apparently, it wasn't their most acclaimed performance, but Brian Epstein and the Beatles were confident they had done enough to secure a contract with Decca. However, as Dick Rowe, the head of A&R at the company, later remembered, "The label was also considering a group called 'Brian Poole and the Tremeloes' who'd also auditioned that same day."

"I told Mike he'd have to decide between them. It was up to him—The Beatles or Brian Poole and the Tremeloes." He said, "They're both good, but one's a local group, the other comes from Liverpool." Therefore, they decided it was safer taking the local group from Dagenham which they felt they could work with more efficiently and stay closer in touch.

It was March 1962 when Decca informed The Beatles they were not required. What really angered Epstein and The Beatles was Rowe's official and now-notorious reason: "Guitar groups are on the way out, Mr Epstein." Yet the Tremeloes were, of course, also a guitar group, and one less talented than The Beatles. Hence Rowe later became infamous as 'the man who turned down The Beatles'.

Fortunately, Brian Epstein persisted: "I told him [Dick Rowe] I was completely confident that these boys were going to be bigger than Elvis Presley." The Beatles were equally unimpressed. In a press interview a few years later, Paul McCartney commented on Rowe's decision, "I bet he's kicking himself." To which John Lennon added, "I hope he kicks himself to death."

The Beatles, however, came away from Decca with reel-to-reel recordings that eventually won the band a deal with the Parlophone label in June 1962 where the head of A&R was George Martin. It was at Parlophone that doubts were raised about Pete Best's drumming skills, and that soon led to Ringo Starr replacing him in The Beatles. If the group *had* been signed by Decca, the individual line-up of The Beatles might have become known as John, Paul, George and Pete!

So, what's the point with persuasion?

Well, of course, we weren't there and may not have been given all the facts about how Decca missed signing The Beatles. Nevertheless, we may want to draw our own conclusions and possibly make some assumptions. With that in mind, perhaps we could conclude that:

- Despite having the most brilliant proposal or idea, this may not be enough on its own to persuade the other person
- We should always be aware of, and never under-estimate, the other parties' likely perceptions
- Being aware of the other parties' needs can help the process of persuasion
- Having a differentiator can be crucial (the only perceived differentiator with The Beatles scenario was that Brian Poole and the Tremeloes had a closer location!)

Decca's rejection of The Beatles was an almost everyday occurrence that many bands would have similarly experienced at that time. Of course, had the decisions taken that day been different, then perhaps the course of music history might have also been entirely different.

British Rail advertising agency

We have learned that persuasion can come in many forms and may be achieved by a variety of methods. Persuasion can be used one-on-one, or in a more complex scenario, when many people need to be persuaded. What we see in all successful acts of persuasion is the use and demonstration of empathy, with the persuader 'actively' seeing things through the other party's eyes.

A remarkable and famous example of this was when a London advertising agency, Allen, Brady, Marsh (ABM), pitched for the British Rail account in 1977.

In the bad old days before the British railway network was broken up into different franchises, or as some would say— dysfunctional rival parts, it operated as a similarly dysfunctional monopoly. Dogged by poor industrial relations, complacent management, government under-investment, a relaxed attitude to punctuality and a casual indifference to customers, British Rail had a severe image problem. To many, it seemed an outdated, under-funded institution, struggling to adapt to changes in the British way of life and the demands of a more savvy customer—the travelling public.

British Rail's chairman, Sir Peter Parker, thought an advertising campaign might do the trick. One of the agencies he invited to tender was Allen Brady Marsh, run by the flamboyant Peter Marsh. He was not an obvious choice, being a cigar-chomping ad man who generally travelled by helicopter.

Sir Peter and a posse of BR's top brass duly turned up at ABM for the pitch at 11.00am. They were received by a bored receptionist filing her nails and made to wait in a dingy foyer, strewn with coffee-stained tables and overflowing ashtrays. With a phone cradled between shoulder and neck, she explained a story to her friend, at some length, about whom she eventually 'went home with' while she continued to file her nails.

Sir Peter politely coughed; she ignored him. He coughed again; she looked up.

"Yes?" she said

Parker responded: **"Excuse me, we're here to see…"**

The receptionist replied: **"Be with you in a minute love."**

Parker (a little irritated): **"But we have an appointment…"**

She ignored him and finished her conversation.

"**Yes, sorry,**" she said, almost apologetically. "**You're the rail people aren't you—Mr Parker isn't it?**"

She continued, "**I'll tell Mr Marsh you're here**" and proceeded to phone 'downstairs' to let him know.

After some while, a girl arrived from 'downstairs' with a Formica tray containing five plastic cups, sachets of sugar (now wet from spilt coffee!), plastic spoons and a small cardboard milk carton with the top roughly torn off.

"**Help yourself,**" she told the BR chairman and his team before leaving them to continue waiting.

Minutes ticked by and still nobody came to meet them.

The chairman said: "**This is outrageous. We've been waiting fifteen minutes.**"

The receptionist replied: "**Can't help that love.**"

Parker, now angry countered: "**Right, that's it, we're leaving.**"

And the senior management of British Rail began to walk out.

"**Please tell Mr Marsh we were here on time, we have waited for 20 minutes and thank him for his interest in our business, but this is not the agency for us**", and they proceeded to leave.

As they were leaving, the agency chairman (Peter Marsh) clad in full BR uniform complete with cap, whistle and flag burst in and said, "**If you don't like it, why should your passengers?**" (Source: *Marketing Communications* 1993 Smith & Taylor)

He'd been watching everything. After shaking the BR chairman's hand warmly, he said:

"Gentlemen, you've just experienced what the public's impression of British Rail is. Now, if you'll come this way, we'll show you exactly how we're going to turn that around."

Erin Brockovich

The character from the film *Erin Brockovich* is often considered an excellent example of the use of persuasion.

This film from the year 2000 tells the true story of a confident single mother who, in 1993, almost single-handedly brought down a Californian power supply company which was responsible for polluting a city's water system that had caused widespread health problems to city dwellers.

Brockovich's persuasiveness in the courtroom helped the case that was won, and with compensation of $333 million being awarded to the 634 plaintiffs.

The film shows how Brockovich successfully uses empathy in a variety of situations. She is depicted making an emotional appeal by explaining the horrors that the victims had been put through. "These people don't dream about being rich. They dream of being able to watch their kids swim in a pool without worrying that they'll have to have a hysterectomy at the age of 20." Both provocative and evocative, Brockovich stimulated affective empathy whereby she challenged the Power Company's defence team to take on some of the emotions of the victims themselves.

Brockovich was effective, if not brutal, in her assault on the defence lawyers. "Think about what your spine is worth Mr Walker. Or, what might you expect someone to pay for your uterus, Ms Sanchez?" These strong statements compelled the lawyers to imagine themselves as the plaintiffs. Her actions forced the lawyers to empathise, show understanding and to adopt the plaintiffs' perspective. Not only that, but she made her case with the clever use of rhetorical questions! These forced the lawyers to realise just how insulting it had been when they suggested that the plaintiffs would be satisfied with a low settlement.

Although in the beginning of the film Brockovich was suing a doctor in connection with a road traffic accident, she lost the case due to her own courtroom behaviour. However, it seems, by her persistence, she more than made up for this in this David and Goliath / Big Company versus Small Individual contest. Her persuasion, of her boss initially, to take the *pro bono* case and 634 of the town's affected residents to work together, resulted in the substantial $333 million payouts awarded to the plaintiffs.

So, what might the reasons be why Brockovich was so successful in her persuasion?

- She built trust and rapport with all the plaintiffs from the town, who realised that she had their interests at heart and cared, so they backed her all the way
- She understood the needs of the plaintiffs, appealed to the jury, and gave compelling reasons to support her case
- She built her case on facts and evidence, but presented them with strong emotional appeal, instead of relying solely on logic for persuasion

Columbus's 'Big Idea' and how he got support for it

Many theories abound over how Christopher Columbus achieved his 'Big Idea' of sailing off into the deep blue yonder to discover new lands. People had conflicting views and believed that the world was flat, not round. While I am no scholar of that period of history, having read some of the different explanations behind Columbus's voyages, this did shed some light on the subject and taught me not only a few lessons about his powers of persuasion but also blew away a couple of myths.

All the accounts I have read suggest his Big Idea was

connected to a theory that, because he was convinced the world was round, it was possible to set sail from a point on one side and circumnavigate the earth back to where he first set sail.

While he wasn't alone in believing that the world was spherical, some historians now say that while most educated people accepted that it was round, he did have to face considerable abuse from some people. However, according to many historians, Columbus was a stubborn character, and once he got a bee in his bonnet, he made honey from it.

It is suggested by some authors that he had researched the works and writings of other explorers such as Marco Polo. Quite how he managed to gather and validate such information, I will never know.

In his imagination, inspired by those that went before, or perhaps even by the local barmaid, Columbus believed he could cross the Atlantic Ocean and reach China and Japan. Columbus's Big Idea was to prove that his theory of a journey west across the Atlantic to China and Japan in the east was not just feasible—it would be quicker. He theorised that if this turned out to be a shorter or less troublesome route of reaching the affluent markets of eastern Asia than the current voyages around the challenging and stormy Horn of Africa, then he could become a very wealthy man.

He appreciated that to embark on a lengthy voyage of this kind was going to be far beyond his financial means. He was also aware that if he succeeded in his quest, he would need the power and authority to keep a healthy slice of the action. But, as a one-man-band adventurer he had very little money and neither the power or the authority. Undeterred, to even attempt his Big Idea Columbus knew he had to find the money, power and authority from one of Europe's royal courts. His answer was to persuade the monarch of a prominent kingdom to come on board (sorry for the pun) by backing his Big Idea.

In 1483, although he was an Italian, Columbus approached the Royal Court of Portugal and presented his idea to King John II who rejected him. The King's decision was reached after conferring with other explorers and mariners favoured by the Royal Court who advised him that Columbus's idea was unthinkable and unrealistic.

You remember that Columbus had a stubborn streak and was therefore not prepared to back down without a fight. So he decided to visit King Ferdinand and Queen Isabella of Spain. This was probably not a random choice. Portugal, despite being a far smaller country than Spain, was well ahead in the race to colonise various parts of the world during that period.

The lesson to be learned from Columbus's actions is this: if No.1 in your market rejects your Big Idea, then take it to their main competitors, No.2. If that fails go to No.3.

In Columbus's case, he believed that his Big Idea could help Spain's Royal House to 'get one over' on its rivals, allowing them to catch up and surpass Portugal in the 'Premier League Table of Seafaring Nations'.

The first attempt by Columbus to persuade Ferdinand and Isabella of the benefits to Spain did not go spectacularly well by all accounts! Queen Isabella was said to have been quite impressed with Columbus, both as a man and by his presentation, although this was insufficient to offer him the backing he needed. While the King and Queen did not reject his proposal, they had questions regarding Columbus's theory that required answering and kept him hanging around for years with vague promises of support. After taking further time to think and consult with others, it seemed they returned to him each time with yet more questions!

Poor old Columbus must have been almost at his wits' end,

but he didn't waste his time entirely. He was, after all, asking for a significant return for his efforts of exploration as part of this Big Idea. In modern-day parlance, he was demanding a hefty day rate, probably way above the minimum wage at the time, and he also requested a list of other lucrative benefits be included within his employment 'package'.

The demands he made to the King and Queen included:

- One-tenth of all the wealth (gold, spices, textiles, slaves and more) that he brought back to Spain from wherever he discovered
- Money for himself and his heirs for posterity for every trip he made to the new lands
- He required being afforded the title of 'Viceroy' of any new territories that he discovered
- And last, but not least... he insisted on being called 'Admiral of the Ocean Seas'

After many attempts at persuading the King and Queen, in April 1492 Columbus was granted a signed contract guaranteeing him all that he desired.

Some act of persuasion, eh?

Before we discuss the lessons on persuasion to be learned from Columbus, there are a couple of myths relating to this story that I was prepared to believe before carrying out research for this book and that have since been reversed.

1. Was Columbus motivated by the desire to prove the world was flat or round?

Many historians now say that few people at that time still believed the world was flat. Indeed, in scientific circles, that idea had already been discredited. From what I can gather, Columbus was driven by the money, power and fame that would go with discovering a new, shorter and more accessible trade route to Asia by sailing west instead of east. He may have had the desire to prove that the world was small. Unfortunately, he made several incorrect assumptions about what he perceived to be the size of the earth. His voyage, therefore, confirmed that our planet is much larger than any experts at that time could ever have imagined.

Columbus did not find the shortcut he believed existed, a situation many of us can empathise with. Instead, he discovered the Caribbean, then inhabited by some interesting people with little in the way of gold, silver, textiles or spices.

2. Columbus persuaded Queen Isabella to sell her jewels to finance the trip

During the time of Columbus, King Ferdinand and his wife, Queen Isabella, had plenty of money. Not that long before, they had secured the Moorish kingdoms in southern Spain and absorbed the wealth from those regions as their own.

While buying three ships, paying for the crews to sail them and the supplies needed for such a trip was beyond the means of Columbus, the King and Queen had a surplus of second-hand vessels at their disposal. Although unclear, at least to me, it is difficult to understand why the royal couple made poor old Columbus wait so long before agreeing to finance his voyage? Perhaps it was connected to the very sizable demands Columbus was making? However, in the end, Columbus proved that his powers of persuasion were stronger than any objections they may have had, and he could no longer be ignored.

What can we learn about persuasion from Columbus and his Big Idea?

1. He did his research as best he could even though we now know that his theory of finding a shorter route to the East was wrong, yet nobody was aware of that then, least of all the royals.
2. He believed in his Big Idea. So much so that he gave up much of his life to pursue his project, researching, persuading, waiting, presenting, being ridiculed, and finally following through and sailing out into uncharted waters.
3. He didn't give up at the first refusal for funding. Some reports suggest he also approach the royals in England as well as Portugal before turning his attention to Spain.
4. He found a link between his Big Idea and the strategic ambitions of the King and Queen of Spain. They wanted to discover a shorter and more accessible trade route too, at least as much as Columbus did. As a result, they were prepared to give him 10% of the wealth generated in perpetuity.
5. He made a great impression on the critical decision-makers. The Queen liked him. And it has often been said that if you want a man to do something, then a straightforward way to achieve this is to get his wife on your side.
6. He made an excellent presentation. He may not have had PowerPoint at his disposal, but by all accounts he did a great job.
7. Lastly, he knew what his Big Idea was worth, and he held his nerve and stood his ground during years of negotiation and refused to be dissuaded or deflected by the delaying tactics of the other side.

The campaign to abolish slavery

We readily accept that news today is instant: television, radio, Twitter, Facebook, and the ubiquitous Google. Many of us are just as much 'makers of the news' as consumers of it. In comparison, the origins of the campaign to abolish slavery began in the 1700s, at a time when most of the world's population knew little about what was happening in the next town or village, let alone on slave ships and plantations across the other side of the globe.

The only media that existed then were newspapers and not everyone could read. The earliest newspaper was a 'weekly' published in Germany in 1605 by Johann Carolus, with the first English newspaper, *The Oxford Gazette*, not appearing until 60 years later. The pioneering press could hardly reflect the views and interests of their readers as they do today considering that, in the 1700s, it is estimated that more than 50% of the UK population could not read. Most people, even if they were literate, didn't have the money to buy newspapers, so readership was pretty much the preserve of members of the ruling classes who were able to read.

Of course, people from all levels of society would have enjoyed the fruits of slavery whether they approved of the practice or not. Commodities such as cotton, tea, rum and sugar were all dependent on slave labour. Few, if any, would have any idea of how these items were produced or at what horrific human cost. Those who did know were the very individuals who were earning a wage from, or generating significant profits, by promoting this inhuman trade and thus retained a personal stake in the slave trade remaining just as it was.

The Act which ended slavery also included the right of compensation awarded to slave-owners who would be losing their property. The UK government paid out over 40,000 separate claims from a £20 million fund set aside for that purpose. This is equivalent to over £2,239,198,484 (£2,238 million) at 2017 rates; 40% of the annual expenditure of the government of the time. In 2017 overall government spending in the UK was £780 billion. Can you imagine trying to persuade Parliament today to spend 40% of taxpayers' money (over £312 billion—almost double what is spent annually on the NHS, some £124 billion) on just one item of expenditure?

When set in this context, the campaign to persuade those who were unaware of what was going on, as well as those knowingly opposed to slave reform, was surprisingly effective.

The slave trade was abolished by the British Empire in 1807, and slavery itself ended in 1833. It is fair to say that the continuation of slavery was influenced by lower-priced goods becoming available from nations such as Brazil and the East Indies, although the slave rebellions in Haiti and Jamaica, amongst others, eventually made slavery unprofitable. Slavery was also unpopular with the public and led to a political uproar in Britain. Despite this, the law still had to be changed, a vote had to be won and those in power, who at first opposed such a change, had to be persuaded to support it.

This required intensive campaigning over a prolonged period. To successfully end slavery, the abolitionists needed to do three things: educate people as to what was going on, persuade them to change their consumer habits, and convince those with the power to change the law. How did they achieve this?

Organising action groups

The Committee for the Abolition of the Slave Trade was formed in 1787 with 12 men: nine Quakers and three Anglicans, to ensure a broader appeal and more significant political influence. Later, William Wilberforce was recruited as the voice of the movement in Parliament.

Quaker meeting houses across the UK were used to raise funds, encourage public involvement, and spread information. By 1780 some ex-slaves who had gained their freedom formed their own movement, The Sons of Africa, and collaborated with other abolitionists. Working in a more organised way allowed the abolitionists to draw on people with a wide range of skills and knowledge to advance the cause.

Investigation and research

The movement faced fierce opposition from those who had made vast fortunes from the slave trade and had the power to lobby or buy politicians. They depicted slavery as legitimate employment by claiming slaves benefitted from life on the plantations, and by arguing that there was no alternative to the use of slave labour.

The abolitionists realised that they had to gather hard evidence to prove this was not true. The researchers and writers used facts impartially rather than by employing emotional, religious or moral arguments. The evidence unearthed included accounts from ships' doctors, traders and British sailors. The abolitionists also published eyewitness accounts, some of which became best-selling autobiographies.

Using a variety of media

The anti-slavery movement was remarkable in that it got vast numbers of the British people to join the cause. This was due to the efforts of the campaigners who got their message across to the entire population, rather than to just a narrow part of it. This was achieved by employing different communication channels, in various ways, to reach target audiences. The campaigners wrote complex proposals to persuade politicians and produced more straightforward messages for the public in an easy-to-read style with graphic posters and guides.

Because less than half the population could read, the abolitionists found other means of spreading their message. Some campaigners travelled extensively, giving impassioned speeches to as many groups as possible in halls and churches and at outdoor events. Other campaigners went door-to-door, particularly during the sugar boycott campaign in the 1820s, calling at hundreds of thousands of homes.

Giving the campaign an identity

Today, the brand is everything and a brand logo with a strapline is used as a powerful symbol on every kind of marketable commodity. The abolition campaign saw the start of this.

In 1787 the campaigners had a seal made depicting a powerful image of an African man, kneeling and in chains with the slogan 'Am I not a Man and a Brother?' Wedgwood, the pottery company, produced a medallion brooch using the same image which was adopted as a fashionable accessory by sympathisers. The model was soon deployed to brand items other than publications and banners, appearing on cufflinks, snuffboxes, tea sets, hat pins, brooches and bracelets.

The most important image was a drawing that showed slaves being loaded onto a ship that was packed so tightly that it was hard to comprehend the sheer inhumanity. This shocking depiction, showing 482 slaves crammed like sardines in a tin can, became the defining image in the battle to end the slave trade.

Obtaining support from the media and influential people

Strong public support helped to drive the campaign forward, but the campaigners still needed to reach the decision-makers and persuade them to act in their favour. It was necessary not to restrict the campaign to any single political party or group if it was to be moved forward by influential people among several crucial stakeholder groups. These included politicians, wealthy businessmen and industrialists, journalists, lawyers and religious leaders.

Lobbying those in power

Another tool first used by the abolitionists was the mass petition. Submitting petitions to Parliament clearly demonstrated the strength of public opinion and showed just how many people opposed the slave trade. The first primary campaign was in 1787-88 when more than 100 petitions containing 60,000 signatures were presented to Parliament in just three months. By 1792, the activists had submitted 519 petitions with over 390,000 signatures, showing that public opinion was massively turning against the slave trade.

Inspiring consumer action

The slave trade flourished because a market existed for products created using enslaved labour. These included rum, cotton, tobacco, coffee and, specifically, sugar. The abolitionists' mission was to convince everyone to understand that the profits from the sugar they used in their tea and cakes was influential in keeping the slave trade alive.

An anti-sugar pamphlet was published in 1791 and ran to 25 editions. Spurred on by pamphlets and posters, by 1792 it was estimated that 400,000 people in Britain were boycotting slave-grown sugar. Grocers reported slave-sugar sales had dropped by more than a third in only a few months. Some people managed without, others used sugar from the East Indies, Cuba or Brazil, especially when they realised it was cheaper. During a two-year period, the sale of non-slave sugar increased ten-fold.

Legal challenges through the courts

Many Africans brought to Britain tried to become free by running away but were pursued by their former masters. The courts were used, both to protect them from being forced back into slavery and to challenge the legality of slavery in Britain. The first challenge came a long time before the organised campaign in 1690 when one slave challenged her master's right to her labour in a county court. She was successful, and the judge granted her the right to leave her cruel owner, who had beaten her and thrown her out, and go to work for another employer.

The limitations of this protection were however demonstrated in 1783 when a prosecution for murder against the captain of a slave ship was dismissed. The judge ruled that the dispute was an insurance claim, and not murder, despite clear evidence that 132 slaves had been deliberately thrown overboard. Even though the case was lost, it highlighted the injustice of the trade and convinced many influential people that it was the law itself that required changing.

Supporting synergistic political reform

A significant obstacle to the abolition movement was the influence of the pro-slavery supporters in the Houses of Parliament. Many parliamentary constituencies, especially those with small electorates, were under the control of wealthy landowners who used their influence to sway local voters and buy their way into Parliament.

The abolitionists realised the need to campaign for the election of members who were both sympathetic to the cause and political reform because it was clear by then that Parliament had to be reformed before abolition could occur.

In 1832 The Great Reform Act proposed wide-ranging changes to the electoral system. It was passed only after significant public pressure, the threat to flood the Lords with new pro-members and pressure from the King himself. The Act granted seats in the House of Commons to representatives of large cities that had developed during the Industrial Revolution and took away seats from those with tiny populations. It also increased the number of individuals entitled to vote to one-in-five of the population.

The abolitionists then campaigned to get those who supported abolition elected. Lists were circulated advising voters whether a candidate was in support of abolition or not. The December elections of 1832 swept away half of those members that had supported slavery from Parliament, paving the way for the 1833 act.

In summary

Combining this range of powerful channels with persuasive factual arguments and haunting images produced radical shifts in thinking across many nations, not just the UK.

When, in recent times, have we seen consumers rapidly desert a commodity used daily for one reason or another? Sales of top brands can drop off a cliff within weeks these days if a negative story goes viral. However, in those days, despite the public's expressed desire to abolish slavery, the system of government had not yet been changed to enable the people's will to be represented fairly in Parliament. Can you really imagine any group persuading such changes in Parliament today? Or the UK taxpayer forcing the government to spend over £312 billion (40% of its annual budget) on a single cause?

A pretty strong case of persuasion, don't you think?

Why did women get the vote?

Seen as a major tipping point in the life of men and women throughout the UK, if not the entire world, getting agreement from the 100% male-dominated political elite was a supreme act of persuasion.

While the origins of equal rights for women had begun a generation earlier, in the UK at least, the campaign for women's suffrage only gained momentum during the early part of the 19th century. At that time, women became increasingly politically active, particularly during the battles to reform suffrage in the United Kingdom. John Stuart Mill, who was elected to Parliament in 1865, was a known advocate of female causes and actively campaigned for an amendment to the Reform Act. This was to include female suffrage, but unsurprisingly, this was heavily defeated in the all-male Parliament.

There were at least three primary forces at work that together created this monumental shift in our society. It is probably hard to think of it as that dramatic today, and yet without it, our whole world would be a very different place.

The three main forces at work were:

- The work of the women's movement known as the suffragettes
- The work of the men, identified as suffragists, who supported this ideal
- The changes brought about by the First World War

The contribution from the suffragists was arguably the least effective, especially in the beginning, as those in power at the time were all men. And, as only men were entitled to vote, this meant that Members of Parliament were only ever likely to remain men unless somebody could force a change. It continued like this until the point when one brave man put forward a motion that began a campaign to gain the support from other men who eventually voted in favour of women having a say.

The main force of persuasion nevertheless came from women, those who believed in this ideal (yet history shows that not every woman did). During the second half of the 19th century several campaign groups were formed, mostly by women, with the intent of lobbying the Members of Parliament to persuade them to support the 'votes for women' movement

In 1897, 17 of these groups united to form the National Union of Women's Suffrage Societies (NUWSS), who held public meetings, wrote letters to lobby politicians, and published various leaflets that were distributed as widely as possible.

In 1907, the NUWSS organised its first significant march. This became known as the Mud March when more than 3,000 women trudged through the cold, wet and rutted earthen streets from Hyde Park to Exeter Hall in London. The movement, its message and its efforts to persuade others, was becoming increasingly popular both with women and men. Unfortunately, the media, which was also wholly male controlled, was less enthusiastic and quickly grew bored with the whole affair, hence reporting was sporadic.

In 1903 some members of the NUWSS had broken away. Led by Emmeline Pankhurst, they formed the Women's Social and Political Union (WSPU) that wanted to use more provocative methods to create publicity for their cause.

This began in 1905 at a meeting where Sir Edward Grey, a member of the newly-elected Liberal government, was speaking at a public event. As he was talking, two members of the WSPU continually shouted: "Will the Liberal Government give votes to women?"

When they refused to cease calling out, police were called to evict them, and two suffragettes were involved in a struggle which ended when both were arrested and charged with assault. After refusing to pay their fines, they were sent to prison for one week and three days. This finally roused media interest and the great British public took notice and was shocked at the suffragettes' use of violence.

After this media success, the WSPU's tactics became increasingly violent. They included an attempt in 1908 to storm the House of Commons, the arson of David Lloyd George's country home and the imprisonment, hunger-strike and force-feeding of suffragettes.

Three Conciliation bills were put before the House of Commons by suffragists, one in each of the years 1910, 1911 and 1912. These laws were designed to extend the rights of women to vote in the United Kingdom of Great Britain and Ireland to around 1,000,500 wealthy, property-owning women. Not every woman—just a start…

On each occasion, further political pressure or concern defeated the bill.

1910—With the Liberals in power, it was feared most of the new voters would be Conservative supporters which would cause the Liberals to lose the next election.

1911—The bill got support with 255 votes to 88 only for it to be overturned by the prime minister who wanted it changed to a 'manhood suffrage bill', the amendment to which would allow just some women to vote. This new variation became buried in red tape and never reached the light of day.

1912—This time the bill was defeated 208 to 222. The main reason was that the Irish Parliamentary Party believed that the time given over to debating votes for women could be used to prevent the discussion required to establish Irish Home Rule.

After this, the WSPU used increasingly violent and more extreme methods to secure publicity for their campaign causing them to lose much widespread support. One notable event was in 1913, when Emily Davison, a suffragette, protested by interfering with a racehorse owned by King George V during the running of the Epsom Derby. After being trampled on by the horse, she died four days later.

When World War I broke out, the WSPU ceased their militant activities and agreed to assist with the war effort. With so many men being sent to France to fight in that appalling war, there were insufficient men left in the UK to work in the fields and the factories. Without food and ammunition no army can fight, so the women took over the mantle by undertaking work customarily done by men. As it turned out, the women produced better results, both in quantity and quality, than their male counterparts even though nobody, at first, thought they could.

This gained the respect of many men including those in the seats of power. In many respects, the exemplary work the women were doing to maintain the war effort was what it took to encourage the politicians to support the idea that women should be entitled to vote.

While the WSPU stopped their militant activities, the National Union of Women's Suffrage Societies, which had always employed more conventional methods to get noticed, continued to lobby during the war years and compromises were reached between the NUWSS and the coalition government. On 6 February, the Representation of the People Act 1918 was passed, enfranchising women over the age of 30 who met minimum property qualifications allowing around 8.4 million women to gain the vote.

What can we learn about persuasion from this?

Asking those in power to give up some of their authority was an amazingly challenging scenario that changed British society for good as well as for the better.

In 1999 *Time Magazine* named Emmeline Pankhurst as one of the 100 Most Important People of the 20th Century, stating: "She shaped an idea of women for our time; she shook society into a new pattern from which there could be no going back."

Persuading one person is challenging enough, but to convince hundreds, let alone hundreds of thousands, is exponentially harder. Persuading someone to accept a proposal that will immediately provide them with benefits can still be a difficult challenge. To transfer this to a group of influential people, by persuading a government that you demand change purely because it is 'right and proper to do so' without offering anything of tangible value in return—is indeed a significant act of persuasion.

Did the violence of the WSPU swing the balance? In the end no; there were plenty of other violent and militant acts taking place in 1910, 1911 and 1912. The suffragettes' actions, by themselves, did not win them the vote, and there is some evidence to suggest that their militancy lost them more supporters than they gained.

We can learn more about the principles of persuasion by studying the reasons why the Act was turned down on three occasions rather than by analysing the actual content of the proposal. As it turned out, the concept of women voting was not the real cause of it being turned down.

Yes in 1910, the Liberal MPs feared the new voters, any new voters. Of course, they didn't want to lose their jobs, but in 1912 it was an entirely different ideal, that of the topic of Irish Home Rule competing for precious time in Parliament, which caused the Bill's defeat.

This shows that you always need to learn to look out for external competing forces that could derail your best effort and ideas.

Did the conventional persuasive methods of the NUWSS win the day? No, not on their own, but it is right to say that without the continued lobbying and dialogue nothing would have changed. And yet, it demonstrated that something else had to occur to alter the response of those in power.

What changed things, in fact, was the War. Sometimes, for our acts of persuasion to work, the environment we are operating in must change. A new MD takes up the post, a new regulation comes into force or an incident happens in a local, national or global sense—all are examples of factors that can influence changes in the way things are valued.

In the case of the suffragettes, a change in the environment combined with decades of lobbying and years of sacrifice, including some extreme incidents, by many women from all levels of society, combined to create an unstoppable proposal.

Modern vote buying

Throughout this book we have been looking at various methods and approaches that can be employed for moral persuasion. What is moral persuasion? According to one definition, it is 'appealing to the ethical principles or beliefs of an adversary, or the public, to convince the adversary to change behaviour or attitudes'. Appealing to the principles or beliefs, of course, implies understanding the person you are trying to persuade in the first place. This relates to what their policies or expectations might be so that the methods of persuasion you are using will appeal to them.

The case study that follows is not an example of moral persuasion in any way, but it can be described as cynical persuasion. It is a 'form' of persuasion, but it lacks morals, and it is a method that we do not advocate in any sense. But it is a form of persuasion nevertheless. Therefore it is useful to understand where lines may be drawn in the sand in life regarding what is acceptable and unacceptable.

In fact, although it is a form of persuasion that brings about the result that one-person desires, it is probably better described as manipulation. We are referring to the practice of vote buying that exists in some countries and cultures. In some nations, this form of manipulation is more widely accepted than in others, yet because it exists and is alive and well, it cannot be ignored.

Vote buying examples

In parts of Africa some politicians move from household to household asking for votes, and they leave a 'tip' at each home visited to try and persuade the citizens to vote in their favour. It is very common, and the vote-buying process can also be in the form of healthcare services that might include offering free immunisation in return for votes. Electoral treating (providing cash payments or other prizes) remains common in some parts of the world, including Africa, and it is still legal at the time of writing in some American jurisdictions such as in the Seneca Nation of Indians of New York.

In recent years, Liberian politicians have been accused of bribing voters. There have been reports in the Liberian media that potential voters were given cash inducements to 'encourage' them to register in electoral districts other than their own:

> *Liberia: Over L$1Million Bribery Claim - 20 January 2011*
>
> *"Days after the Nimba County Junior Senator Adulphus Dolo made a stunning revelation that he was the middleman in striking a one million dollar deal aimed at convincing the Standard Bearer of the National Union for Democratic Progress (NUDP), Sen. Prince Y. Johnson to give up his political ambition and join the ruling Unity Party, the Chairman of NUDP, Mr. Emmanuel Lormack, has broken ice on the matter, claiming that statements attributed to the Nimba Lawmaker are a bunch of twaddle, The Analyst reports.*

The NUDP national Chairman, Mr. Emmanuel Lomax, addressing scores of Journalists at his NUDP's office denied that his party was ever part of such 'crocky' deals as alleged by Senator Dolo, claiming that he never signed any secret document on behalf of the party, least to let go what he termed as the anxiety in liberating the Liberian people.

Mr Lomax argued that though the Unity Party on several occasions made offers for the political bargaining chip, but said the NUDP had since refused to give room to the offers from the UP on the grounds that doing so would be considered in the NUDP's view "a bid to rob politicians and political parties of their constitutional duties."

In Kenya it seems that the practice of vote buying is also regarded as acceptable in some parts. One story from a news agency read: *"Voters rough up a man alleged to have been bribing voters at the Musoli voting centre during today's by-elections in Ikolomani. Speaking about what promises to be a hotly contested election next year, President Mwai Kibaki recently advised Kenyans to 'eat politicians' money if it is offered', but to vote with their heads."*

Of course, vote buying is not a new practice—it has been with us for hundreds of years. The most famous episodes of vote buying came in 18th century England, with the 'Spendthrift election' that took place in Northamptonshire in 1768, when three earls spent over £100,000 each to win a seat.

Voters may also be given money or other rewards for voting in a specific way, or for not voting in some cases. In some jurisdictions, the offer of providing cash payments or other prizes is referred to as electoral treating. Vote buying may also be done indirectly, for example, by paying clergymen to tell their parishioners to vote for a specific party or candidate.

The idea that money does NOT always buy you the heart of the person suggests that it is more about manipulation rather than moral persuasion, where you connect with the person and appeal emotionally. Thus, if you own a shop or a pub, you will take the customer's money, sell them what they want, but you may still detest that customer. In the prostitution industry, a sex worker doesn't have to love the men she sells her services to. In fact, she wouldn't be able to function if she did. Therefore a prostitute must remain detached from her clients. One famous tale attempts to explain this:

A Catholic and a Protestant bishop appeared on a TV talk

show. The presenter asked the Protestant bishop if he would accept an offer to rehabilitate the church from money donated by a prostitute. The Protestant bishop was outraged. "That is money made from sin, it is dirty, I would never accept it", he said.

The Catholic bishop was then asked the same question. He said: "Who am I to judge the Lord's plan? All things on Earth are put there by God. It is he who knows best. Therefore, I would take the money."

Although vote buying is not really persuasion in a sense we have established in this book, it is a practice nevertheless that some might regard as having some merits. By allowing a market for votes makes it clear what many already know—that money influences politics.

A US journalist, James Stacey Taylor, wrote about the forthcoming presidential elections in an online blog on New Jersey (NJ.com) in 2012 by stating that there is a good argument for vote buying.

"With the national elections just weeks away, the campaigns of both President Obama and former Massachusetts Gov. Mitt Romney are ramping up their efforts to persuade citizens to give them their votes. But rather than spend millions of dollars trying to persuade citizens to vote for them, it would be far more sensible for them to be allowed to buy votes from people who wanted to sell them.

Lest you think I'm facetious, consider the status quo: Our money currently is taken from us via taxes and used to influence policy, and we don't even get a few dollars for our votes in return. In an ideal world, politicians wouldn't have this power at all. But since they do, we might as well get something for our vote.

The economic logic here is simple: If a person sells his vote, he would be made better off by the transaction, for he preferred what was being offered to his vote. The politician who bought the vote would also be made better off, for he would prefer the votes to the items or cash they exchanged for them."

Taylor claims there are 'reasonable arguments' against vote buying—but according to an article he wrote, none shows that a market in buying votes should be outlawed.

The fact that vote buying isn't moral persuasion is picked up by Taylor in his article when he says: "rather than trying to persuade citizens to vote, it would be more sensible to buy votes".

So, what's the point?

- Vote buying is a widely used tool today in many social classes for gaining behaviour change—but it isn't persuasion
- Vote buying doesn't connect with a person and appeal to their interest and their emotions—but moral persuasion does
- Vote buying buys short-term commitment, 'the then and the now', while moral persuasion tends to secure long-term commitment

The only way to gain genuine commitment is through involvement, and vote buying doesn't allow for that. Moral persuasion does.

SUMMARY

In this chapter we have attempted to highlight principles and lessons on the skills and art of persuasion by introducing you to some classic examples: some real, some from the world of film and TV, some that worked exceptionally well and some that failed miserably. In the case of the *Argument* sketch, this will have also brought a level of mischief and hilarity to the commentary. What we have shown is that we can all learn successful approaches, tools and skills from many experiences beyond our own. We found it difficult to restrict the content to just a few examples where persuasion has played a part because there are so many cases. Spread over the history of mankind, there are many thousands of relevant stories that are considered significant because of their capacity to teach us, not necessarily because they worked so well.

In some small way we hope that this chapter, in its brief coverage of the film that featured Erin Brockovich's struggle, how the slave trade was ended, the Beatles' contract was lost, and the British Rail advertising contract won, has inspired you to search beyond just your own life for other applications of the art and skill of persuasion. Because, if from now on you are prepared to look at every successful advertising campaign (as well as at every one that seriously flops), at every business negotiation you are involved with, and at every film you watch, you will intentionally seek out more lessons on persuasion. If you do this and learn from the experiences, then our job is done, and your success is pretty much assured. However, do not forget, you will only reap the benefits of these experiences by applying what you continue to learn.

Some acts of persuasion may take your entire lifetime, involve many people and even changes in the law. Some may be concluded in a flash once you offer a special incentive. Other examples of persuasion may require a level of credibility that you can only gain through a period of backbreaking work, or by seeking significant referrals from those with royal connections!

As we said at the beginning of this book, we all have a need to persuade at some point or other throughout our lives. So, we hope you can take inspiration from the famous and infamous acts of persuasion we have included within the text and apply enough of the wisdom contained within them to improve and enhance your own skills... and ultimately your life.

REFLECT AND LEARN

What ideas did you take from this chapter that were original, fresh, or new to you? What teaching was familiar? In what ways do you already apply some of this learning?

How did you react emotionally and cognitively to the ideas in this chapter? What concepts do you agree with and why? What do you disagree with and why?

What were the most exciting or useful insights gained from reading and thinking about this chapter?

In what ways might you translate the ideas presented throughout this chapter into practical, useful, everyday ideas and plans?

What new questions about persuasion do you now have after reading this chapter?

ACTION LEARNING

In addition to the three original examples you selected at the beginning of the book, list several other people that might benefit from what you have learned about persuasion.

Set yourself some time-phased goals to apply what you have learned that you listed in the Reflect and Learn section; some goals to guide your actions over the next three months, the next three weeks and the next three days.

Thinking about how you plan to apply your learning, what obstacles might you encounter along the way? And, realistically, how might you deal with them?

Who else could you share these ideas with as a supportive sounding board or informal coach? How might you go about setting up a conversation with them to enrol them in supporting your application of this teaching? What might be some of the reasons that would persuade them to become involved? How might they also benefit?

6

Case Studies and Applications

Case studies

Here is a true-life case study from Mal Jones

Are you safer with or without a written contract?

"I took a six-month interim role as a procurement advisor to a company in the health sector, working directly with the Purchasing Director. It was apparent very early in the position that the director wasn't in favour of written contracts; he believed there was little risk in verbal agreements, even though his company was experiencing supply performance problems with some of their suppliers. Coincidentally part of my role was to 'sort out the suppliers and improve the performance'.

I tried to get behind the reasoning for the director's view and approach, getting to grips with his concerns. I knew that the company I was working for was accepting some supplier contracts where the emphasis was on the supplier's terms and conditions rather than ours. I needed to understand the reasoning behind the director's reluctance to manage risk and performance through producing written agreements based on our needs and preferences.

I spoke to the other members of the purchasing team. It was interesting to understand that my other colleagues had a different view from our director. In discussions with them, it was clear that they, like me, believed that contracting with suppliers using their own company terms and conditions would provide improvements to their working relationship with those same suppliers.

Purchasing team members also needed a consistent reference point when dealing with suppliers. Personnel changes on both sides would have little impact on contract performance because whoever came in would have a written brief of the contractual expectations. At the contract renewal stage or when a change was required there would always be a consistent base to start from. The purchasing team wanted to use their own company contracts, instead of the suppliers', so that they were in control of terms and conditions which enabled them to manage the risk on behalf of their company.

I spoke to the internal customers inside the company who felt the full effect of poor supplier performance. They were consistently complaining to the purchasing director about one supplier or another and felt no progress was being made to improve things.

While interviewing the internal customers of the company, it was clear that they would value copies of the specification of the contract, the delivery terms and of the performance criteria they as customers, or end users, felt had already been established in their conversations with the purchasing team. The internal customers all agreed a contract written by our company clarifying those essential elements provided fact, rather than opinion on performance criteria, and so was good for everyone involved.

I went to get a view from the suppliers, particularly those performing poorly according to our people, to understand their difficulties and asked why they thought they had moved from being an excellent supplier to a poorly performing supplier.

Interviewing the suppliers consistently demonstrated a desire from them to have a written specification, agreed on performance levels and critical deliverable criteria. A contract to the supplier meant continuity of tenure (12, 24 months, etc). They would understand what was expected regarding quality, delivery, packaging and presentation. They would know the payment terms. They would know the penalties for poor performance, and they would be able to show the contract detail to their internal teams so that everyone at their company understood the implications of the agreement. All the suppliers expressed the view that a written contract was even-handed, protecting them as much as protecting the customer.

I left the interview with the purchasing director until last, so that I had gathered the information from all the people who felt the impact of his approach. The director thought he and his team should be working on the 'trust' approach with suppliers and didn't want the bureaucracy of contract production and the administration that went with it. The director apparently didn't like the problem calls from customers about supplier performance either.

I was able to put to him the reaction from his suppliers and the view that they would appreciate formal agreements which explicitly set out what they had to deliver. Any performance issues would be discussed around the key deliverables criteria, rather than unsubstantiated complaints. Issues could then be resolved professionally.

I talked him through his customer requirements that they would value actual specification information and performance criteria, so they understood the implication of the agreement on them. They felt that this would reduce the complaints.

I outlined that the director's purchasing team were clearly

requesting a formal approach to supplier management and contracting which gave them a benchmark for performance with their suppliers. They wanted their own standard contract for purchasing goods and services so that they could control terms and conditions and manage risk.

Further to this, I wrote up the interviews, responses, recommendations and suggested next steps, copying in all the people I had interviewed.

Using the feedback, the purchasing director began to see that formal contracting with suppliers provided some critical benefits to his company, his team, his customers and his suppliers:

- Company terms and conditions which managed his company's risk
- Clear performance criteria and critical deliverables between his suppliers and his own business
- The beginnings of a consistent record of all his suppliers' contracts and history
- Fewer supplier performance problems and those that did occur could be managed alongside the performance criteria in the agreement
- Fewer complaints from his customers about poor supplier performance
- Happier suppliers, who knew what they had to deliver against contract
- Improved costs, as the suppliers would negotiate a contract over 12, 24 months, etc
- Customer satisfaction because they knew the performance criteria and critical deliverables
- Purchasing team satisfaction because they were in control of contract risk and supplier performance issues should they occur

The result: the purchasing director set his team the task of producing model contracts for all goods and services contracts with their suppliers. They set up a contract reference library. They began an approach which managed supplier performance against the agreement. They brought customers together with suppliers to discuss performance issues whenever they occurred. They started to work together with their suppliers instead of competing, setting up customer/supplier/purchasing workshops to initiate improvements in working practices which began the process of improving costs and service delivery.

All these initiatives began the process of reducing the risk to the business, improving the specifics of supplier management and providing a positive impact on the bottom-line (profit) of the company. The purchasing director couldn't deny the benefits, and reducing the complaint calls to his office provided the cherry on the cake.

What I learned about persuasion along the way:

1. Planning the approach to tackling any problem provides a route through some of the issues. You do need to believe in the solution and have confidence in a plan or strategy to get there.
2. You need a clear understanding of the other parties' viewpoints, so you need to listen to the principal participants and understand their issues and concerns. This requires the use of open questions: how, why, where, what, who and when to establish the critical issues. Make notes along the way and summarise the key points so you can get a clear, concise picture in your mind.
3. By having a detailed understanding of how the person you are trying to persuade is thinking, allows you to research and find the best solution to any problems. You must ensure

you answer all the issues and address all the arguments even if it means finding creative solutions which will excite the other person.
4. You also must find ways to explain things, ways that will provide the reassurance points to make your proposal feel like the best option and even the safest.
5. Keep the main parties or stakeholders informed while you are doing your homework. The internal customers at the company had up to that point felt like nobody cared. Let people know what you are doing and what stage you are at. The more people or teams or companies involved, then the more critical frequent and accurate information becomes.
6. Finally, ensure your proposal does deliver the WIIFM (what's in it for me), the benefits for all parties. Getting others to buy in, where a return on the investment for everyone involved is clear and tangible, is usually much simpler. Be sure you provide quantifiable 'bottom-line' (profit) solutions wherever possible."

A true-life case study from Eli Shine

An ice cream gets you into the hot seat.

"Being a parent must be one of the best training grounds available for learning about the topic of persuasion. There is probably no better, in fact. If you are like me, your kids do not always want to do exactly what you want them to do, at least when you need them to do it, if at all. Of course, the last thing I wanted to do was make my children scared of me. So, once I had figured out that they weren't (scared that is), I realised that it is pointless getting angry or frustrated with them for having a different preference from mine. Instead, I figured it was the ideal time to use and improve my techniques of persuasion to win them over to my way of thinking.

Until recently, every family trip in our car would usually get off to a slow start. Why? Because although we have a sizeable seven-seat estate car, the air conditioning does not reach all the way to the very back and, as we live in Israel, that can be a problem. At times it gets hot in the back. This means that at least one of our four children must suffer the heat and claustrophobia of the back row most times we go out. And if they know it is a relatively long trip, as you can imagine, we rarely have a volunteer. It used to take a significant number of unpleasant minutes trying to convince one of the children that it was their turn to go in the back. During this time I would have to remind myself to stay calm, remember how to count to ten and smile through clenched teeth.

This went on for a long time until one steamy hot summer's day I decided I didn't have the energy for the fight anymore, so I pulled my youngest daughter (five years old at the time) aside and whispered, "Would you like an ice cream?" Yes, was the quick reply. "Well, here's the deal. If you go in the back both ways today, I'll get you an ice-cream." Her eyes lit up, and she gladly hopped into the back seat without saying a word. The other three gleefully jumped into the other, cooler seats, thinking they had got away with an easy victory.

While I was feeling pleased with myself to begin with, that was not the most significant result I gained from that moment of inspiration. It was what happened next. Our eight-year-old daughter, who always complained of feeling sick in the back to reduce the number of times she got the short straw, caught on, and requested, no, demanded the opportunity to go in the back BOTH ways next time so that she too could qualify for this reward. Now, if two of our girls were getting ice cream, my eldest daughter was not going to be left behind, and so she negotiated the same terms and eagerly awaited her turn to go in the back.

People move away from pain and towards pleasure every time, and not just children. To persuade, we must be able to demonstrate how our proposal is beneficial to the other person, how it gives them something they value (pleasure) or removes something they don't like (pain). It is well worthwhile considering how we can change the total package of what we are offering to make it sweeter for the person being persuaded. Since that fantastic day when I discovered a fundamental principle of persuasion by accident, we travel regularly, often for up to three hours. Now there is no fuss at the beginning and relative peace for up to three hours at a time, all for less than $3 a trip and that is a pretty good deal!"

A true-life case study by Ian Tredaway

One size does not fit all.

"I had to meet a new prospect, the MD of a small recruitment and IT training firm. He was having a hard time and not achieving the reasonable targets he had set. He felt he had a clear need to develop the skills of his sales team.

The essential problem was they did not see enough of the right kind of prospects. Without a precise target customer profile and an ideal lead definition, his team were unable to prioritise who they needed to put the most time into. Overall, they were wasting a lot of sales effort chasing too many of the wrong kind of leads. When they did get to see the better prospect, well in truth any prospect, the sales people were not moving them through to the next step in the sales process quickly enough or often enough—fundamental sales problems that we could have helped them with.

In putting together the proposal for the MD, I used, as ever, a clear principle about pricing. As a sales consultancy, on principle I do not discount. I would not be modelling good behaviour, in my view, by offering different people different levels of discount. I wouldn't be much of a salesperson if I had to lower my price to win business. I believe this approach is fair to everyone. I merely price 'correctly' in the first place, whether it is a project large or small, or a client large or small. I treat everyone the same.

An old human relationship principle is 'treat people the way you wish to be treated' which leads you to treat everyone the same. This principle, along with my pricing policy, had served me well up to this point so why change?

This MD was an astute businessman, intelligent and very knowledgeable in this industry. Regarding his personality he is a big hustler, always on the lookout for a profit here or a margin there, motivated in the main by material success and tuned in tightly to that great radio station WIIFM.

What I should have thought through, this time more than ever before, was that he would want and ask for, if not demand, a 'special deal'—something made just for him.

When I presented my proposal he liked it, it contained the right elements, it showed that I had listened, done my homework on his company's problem and knew my stuff as a sales consultancy. But then when he got to the 'back page' he just looked up and asked for my 'best price'.

I said what I always say on these occasions. I have a strict pricing policy, blah blah, that is fair for everyone, blah blah, and would not budge. The MD got quite annoyed; we both said things to defend our fixed positions and then—shock-horror—I was asked to leave. His final comment as I walked out of his office was "…and don't bother contacting me again".

What I learned is that everybody is different, and while you may be correct in offering everyone the same meat, it generally makes more sense to provide them with their own favourite gravy. A more powerful approach to a human relationship is to treat people the way they wish to be treated. A fair pricing policy for all would appeal to some people while alienating others. It would have been simple to describe the pricing as unique, special and my 'best' in the first place.

To be more persuasive I had to learn to think more about the personality type of the prospect I am dealing with and develop proposals and pricing based on their motivations, not mine. One size most certainly does NOT fit all when it comes to persuasion and influence."

A true-life case study from Kevin Clarke

Unspoken concerns.

"Many years ago (circa 1980) I secured a significant amount of business with the retail group Carrefour UK. Carrefour is a very successful supermarket business in France, even today. Many people will know it well from any 'booze-cruise trips' to Calais. In the late 1970s and early 80s, Carrefour had six or seven hypermarkets dotted around the country, and they were set to expand.

My company at the time, Clarke Packaging, supplied a range of fresh food packaging to about 75% of its stores. I had made a separate arrangement with each of the stores and was doing quite well from it. The purchasing team at Carrefour head office wanted to set up a group deal with one national supplier and take central control. I was in two minds about this potential change—on the one hand, we could win the other 25% of the business that had always eluded our company, and yet on the other, we could lose the lot. This was by far our most extensive account (roughly £500,000 p.a.), one that I, as sales director, controlled. It is fair to say that the nerves in the boardroom at Clarke Packaging were up!

The head of procurement at Carrefour asked the chief accountant at the Birmingham store, a guy called Tim, to take the responsibility of researching all products and deals that each store had set up independently, and to make a recommendation to the board for the most appropriate supplier. That favoured supplier would then be used across the entire group, after being awarded 100% of the food packaging business at Carrefour. The remainder of the suppliers would be locked out of that business for at least three years.

The Birmingham store was one of the few stores our company did not deal with, and so Tim was unknown to me. It was apparent that Tim was going to have a significant say in the outcome as he was the guy doing the presentation to the head of procurement. As no supplier was going to be able to deliver their proposal in person, this meant that, if I was ever going to be able to persuade the head of procurement, I had to find a way to convince Tim that we were the supplier of choice.

However, when I initially spoke to Tim on the telephone, he made it clear he was going to do his homework thoroughly and meet with every supplier, so I felt I had to be first to give Clarke Packaging the best chance of success. For me, face-to-face contact, even today with email and Skype, is still the best option when I need to build rapport and trust quickly. Thankfully it was easy to set up the first meeting. When I met him, I got him talking about his favourite topics: about himself, his business, and his problems. He confessed he needed to do a lot of homework because he had very little knowledge about packaging; why should he—after all, he was an accountant.

Tim's boss had a 'Big Idea'. Not only was Tim to meet with every one of the current suppliers, but he was also to visit each of the stores. During the store visit, he could speak directly to the department heads to learn who and what packaging they used, and, more importantly, why. He could also ask how they would like to see different packaging developed and see for himself any problems the stores were having with its existing packaging. This was a recipe for a great discussion; it was a wonderful idea. With the insights gained from such a tour, Tim's boss would be in a far better position to make sense of each supplier's proposal and could, therefore, make a much better recommendation to Carrefour.

Tim's 'problem' was that he was not used to travelling and he found even the thought of having to visit each of the stores rather daunting. It probably seems crazy to anyone reading this in the age of the satnav and smartphone app that planning and taking such a journey was in any way a problem. But, I am talking about journeys that were made in the 'stone-age'. In the early 1980s you had the AA or RAC printed roadmap to rely on and little else. You also had A4 bound books with an A to Z index of every street known in the area covered with a grid reference to help you find it on the page. Inevitably, by the time any map book was printed, it was already out of date; new roads, changes to one-way systems and the challenge of reading the stupid things while driving was enough to put many people off venturing too far into the unknown.

Of course, regarding persuasion, one person's problem can be the other's opportunity, so I offered to help. I volunteered to drive him on his UK tour because I knew where each store was located and would also be on hand to answer any questions he had relating to any packaging. Most of the packaging used by Carrefour was, in any case, ours, and I would, at least, be able to provide essential information on the 25% that wasn't.

For me this was an excellent opportunity, as I'd have hours in the car with him. We'd be able to talk at length and get to know each other. The understanding and trust we could potentially develop would be significant regarding the future proposal to Carrefour. And after all that time together, he would at least give me a fair chance at winning the business.

I expected him to be wary. It is understandable that the situation could give Clarke Packaging an unfair advantage and, if discovered, he would feel the backlash of disapproval from his boss. And yet, the way he immediately declined, or more the tone of his voice, made me think there was something he wasn't telling me.

It became apparent that he viewed things from his position thus:

- It would give me an unfair advantage
- I could spend the travelling hours 'selling' to him
- If I were with him during the visits to those stores that were my customers, he would not feel able to speak truthfully, especially if they had to make negative comments about my own products or service
- If his boss found out…
- If the other suppliers found out…

I just sensed there was something more he wanted to tell me but wasn't saying. This was only our first meeting, so I laid out my proposal as warmly and fairly as I could:

- As the largest packaging supplier to Carrefour, at that time, I would feel obliged to be at the stores I supplied when he was visiting in case he had questions about our products that only I could answer

- That meant regardless of whether he took up my offer of the lift, I would have to make the exact same journey and be at the same store at the same time
- I would not interfere during a site visit; I would, in fact, leave him in the capable hands of the store manager and wait for him in the office
- In the car, I promised to stick to non-business topics unless he asked a specific question
- I would be discreet about the 'lift' so not even the store managers would know

I also distinctly laid out one painful fact; painful to him at least. I knew how to get to every store, and he didn't. For him learning about the packaging was reasonably straightforward compared to the rigours of traversing the highways and byways that make up the UK road network. I left that point until last, so he had it fixed firmly in his mind as 'something to look forward to'.

Our first meeting had ended with a definite and robust 'no'. He had not moved from the position he had adopted, and I didn't really want to move from mine either. But, I could genuinely help make his research more useful, and I would undoubtedly make his journey less painful. Still, there were plenty of other things for us to discuss because even for a smart accountant, packaging is a specialised area. We agreed to meet the following week. Seven days too long for me, but there seemed to be nothing I could do about that.

At our next meeting, I intentionally focussed on building the rapport and kept the subject matters under discussion away from the tour itself. Instead, I tried to demonstrate a detailed knowledge of packaging which I tried to deliver in an honest and balanced way with the aim of being accepted as a 'trusted advisor' rather than as a 'salesperson'.

When we finally got around to the topic of 'planning the store visits' I again offered to help him conduct his research and make his journeys more productive. This time I presented it more as a question rather than a fixed idea. I asked: "How I could make your research more effective while making the trips a bit easier?"

Instead of answering he explained his real concern, the thing I sensed that went unsaid the last time we had met:

"I know you are trying to help Kevin, but you see I volunteered to do this store research because it will justify my application for a company car. If I must go around all the stores before awarding the national packaging contract, the company need to get me a car. If they do get me a car, and I have to travel over x miles on company business, not only will they pay for all my petrol, but I will also avoid the tax normally due on a benefit-in-kind. Conversely, if I travel with you, then I cannot justify a car unless I am prepared to take a hit on my tax code."

Now I understood his real concern it was easy to find a solution. So, I responded by saying: "Whether you travel in my car or I travel in yours, or you follow me, you in your car and me in mine, I don't really care. Quite frankly I need to be at the same stores when you visit them and travelling alone is boring. I'd really be very glad of the company."

Of course, once this was out in the open, he took up my offer. I never mentioned it to anyone and nor did he. We did get a chance to establish a strong understanding of each other, and while he was very professional, I always knew he would give me a fair chance when it came to his final recommendation to Carrefour.

Did we win the business? Yes, we did, and it was a good deal for both Carrefour and Clarke Packaging. We held that

account until Carrefour was absorbed into the Gateway and Summerfield supermarket chain several years later.
What did I learn from this?
Firstly, it reinforced the value of rapport and trust because if someone does not trust you, then they will not dare to say what is really going on in their head. All you are going to get is a straight emphatic 'no', which you are very unlikely to be able to turn around because you don't know the reasoning behind it.

Secondly, it taught me to listen to my intuition. I knew, or at least sensed, there was something else going on in Tim's head and so had to find a subtle way of teasing it out.

Finally, it taught me that for straightforward proposals to be accepted, they will be those that the other person designs with you. I would never have thought about Tim's desire to have his own company car and his need to clock up high mileage. Only he would have known that."

A true-life case study—Liz Clarke

My whole life is about persuasion because I work in marketing.
"Two years ago, I persuaded 90 customers, staff and board members of three merging organisations to give up two hours of their time. We went through a branding process to create the foundations of the new company.

Together they decided on what the newly merged organisation stands for: its vision, mission and four one-word brand promises that they would commit to living by. My designers developed a powerful visual identity to portray the new organisation and its promises, and we persuaded everyone to adopt the imagery without a problem.

Any agency will tell you that this type of situation can be severe, and it was—but it was all in a day's work for me—it is my chosen profession. Life went on, the organisation continued to raise its profile, and we used the branding exercise as a high-profile case history.

Two years later a bomb exploded, not an actual weapon, just a sudden, unexpected, and disturbing event.

It happened some two years after the organisation had gone to such pains to agree its vision, mission and brand promises. I had just been elected to join its board of voluntary directors. This was a group of influential business people who are each keen to serve the broader local business community. The executive directors asked a small number of the voluntary directors, including me, to join them at an away-day event with the aim of developing a new marketing strategy. It was essential to clarify the policy and to focus on a drive to win more customers in the face of the economic stress and greater competition at that time.

The executives had engaged one of my competitors to facilitate the day. This was only fair and proper because I had theoretically swapped sides and was now a part of the organisation. They had briefed the agency on the plan for the day, and the organisation, as an excellent professional business, had submitted a detailed recommendation. I asked to see the project a week or so before and was horrified by what I saw.

My competitor wanted to spend the morning taking the directors back through an exercise, to re-examine the brand values and consider which were still relevant. These were the values that their customers, staff, and the executive and voluntary directors themselves had agreed as the bedrock on which to build the organisation just two years before.

Now they wanted a small group of us, locked away in private, to look at changing them. I felt that this was both very wrong and a real waste of valuable time. It was also a wasted opportunity because we had to find a new marketing strategy and find a way to win new customers.

What's more, I wasn't even sure the afternoon exercises would get us the required result.

My immediate reaction was one of militancy. Abdicating and refusing to play is not my style, and while I could probably make an acceptable Joan of Arc and fight the impossible fight, the marketing person at my core started to slow down the emotional tide in me so I could think a little more constructively.

Firstly, why did the executive director who briefed the agency think it was a good idea to examine if the brand promises were still relevant? Did that mean they were using the values in running the business and found them to be irrelevant? Or worse yet, had they forgotten the benefits and were failing to refer to them?

I asked for a meeting with the respective executive director, and as I warmed up the atmosphere to tackle the issue, I opened with a few questions about the reasons behind setting the meeting up. I discovered that he was really struggling to get his fellow executives to take any notice of the vision, mission and values beyond the well-chosen words on a pleasantly framed poster. Neither were they sticking to their current marketing strategy, and there was substantial evidence that different people were sending different parts of the business in different directions.

This lack of focus was a contributing factor in the trend of poor results and had to be tackled. Together we went through the plan that the agency had put together, and instead of pointing out what was wrong, I asked more questions, this time as to how each exercise would help us solve the core problem and get the focus back into the team.

After about 20 minutes, he asked if it would be ok if he got the other agency on the speakerphone for me to help him explain to them how he felt much of their recommendation was not fit for purpose. 'Smart move' or something equally supportive, said I.

That call was a simple one—the manager at the other agency willingly agreed to change the plan, only once muttering, "Well, we were only following your brief!"

So, I learned (probably not for the first time, and it won't be the last!) that the art of persuasion has a lot to do with finding out what the other person is thinking. That means asking a fair few questions and getting the other person to 'open up' to explore the topic or topics under discussion. Only then is it wise to proffer an opinion or proposal."

A true-life case study from Mike Kean

Rebuilding a bridge to a dream.

"I was sitting in the front room of my son Christopher's house a year to the day after he qualified as a teacher looking at his lessons plans and a group photograph of his pupils. He was so excited and enthused as he happily described his life as a teacher, pumped up by the opportunity to reach a new generation and inspire their interest in art. I'd never seen him looking so motivated and confident. I thought—boy, this is so different from where we were a little over one year ago.

One year before Christopher had opted out of pretty much everything after a string of problems that started with an accident at home which left him with a deformed arm. After the crash, he chose a hard way to live which stopped him from finishing his degree course. He took to cannabis to release the pressure and nullify the pain. He destroyed much of his artwork in dark periods of depression and anger. He skipped from job to job because he found conflicts with his passionately-held socialist beliefs all around him. He was on a downward spiral compounded by debt and so chose to opt out of most things that had been a part of his life before.

As parents, my wife Mary and I found this period of his life very difficult. Trying to be supportive without interfering; trying to offer advice without being critical. Our initial attempts at persuading him failed miserably, but we could not give up on our own son.

No matter what happens, we were determined to persuade Christopher to finish his degree. I, for one, wanted to say I had at least achieved that one thing in my life.

Mary and I sat down one day and wrote down every excuse he had used ever since the accident in various conversations with us. The writing was difficult for him and the act of painting was painful. Christopher was never going to be able to create physically what he had in his mind. On top of this, he got tired quickly, and people looked at him in a strange way. It was a long list and included many very genuine and practical problems such as his debts and his short fuse when things refused to go his way.

Having written out all the negative aspects of his life, and the many constraints he viewed as impenetrable barriers preventing him living out his previous dream, we started to list all the positives. He had an excellent partner and beautiful little daughter. He had an excellent knowledge in his chosen field of art and a superb eye for detail. He did have a strong desire to teach, but we were not sure if that was now gone.

Mary and I then set about researching answers to as many of the problems as we could, so that we had multiple options for each. We were determined to prove to Christopher that it was still possible to turn his life around with a mixture of short-term steps giving an early sense of progress and some long-term ones, giving a sense of light at the end of the tunnel.

During a visit to his house, we sat him down and got very serious with him. We explained with as much strength and love as we could our desire for him to turn his life around. We explained that we were prepared to help with each and every problem he faced and our belief that they could all be overcome. We showed him our list of solutions which indicated that getting his degree was possible, and 'all' he had to do was to 'man-up', work with us and see his degree course through. We reminded him of his incredibly caring partner and fantastic daughter. We told him of his original ambition to teach and showed him a path back to that dream in the hope he would take the first step.

I'd like to say that he had a 'eureka moment', came to his senses, and we all lived happily ever after, but you know life is not like that. For what felt like a lifetime, each conversation Mary or I had with Christopher was a conscious act of persuasion. Each excuse he made we turned around. For each practical problem, we offered a solution. Each outburst we faced calmly and patiently and waited until he was more reasonable. Each time he looked down we asked him to look up at his partner, his daughter, and his dream.

Christopher did go back to college, and he did see the course through, passing with a creditable 2/2 at the end.

With the first step accomplished we now had to work on getting him into a teacher training college, and with 800 applicants for a limited number of places it was never going to be easy. With our help planning and our encouragement on preparation, he was accepted for the one-year course, but soon after starting his old fears and demons returned and he decided he wanted to drop out.

Mary and I took the same approach as before, and with lots of persuasion, we were able to keep him on the course which he successfully completed. Thankfully he secured his first full-time teaching job straight from college.

To this day he is not interested in his degrees and qualifications, neither the PGCE nor the degree from Edinburgh's St Margaret's College. It is clear though that the thought of teaching children, of reaching out to the next generation and planting the ideals that come alongside a love of art has pumped him up. It was part of his internal motivation that enabled him to turn his life around. I am proud to say he has given up the weed, stopped smoking, does not drink much alcohol and is an excellent father to his daughter and her younger brother.

What did I learn about persuasion in all of this?

Firstly, if you care enough about something that is important, then you are far more likely to persist. Persuasion in many situations is not just a one-off event or conversation, especially if what is at stake is something life-changing for you or for others.

Secondly, the other person, or people, may only be able to see the problems, the difficulties, and the barriers. To them, these may well form an impenetrable wall and as such cut them off from seeing the potential solutions. You may be able to conceive solutions and believe progress is possible and that the difference between both sides can be a vast gap.

Lastly, to build a bridge across that chasm you must plan. Breaking down all of Christopher's issues and problems, real and perceived, was a significant turning point for us all. Once we had that list, we could start to build small solutions and one step at a time get acceptance, and so make progress.

When you can see the potential in others, and you care enough, it is incredible what barriers you can knock down in pursuit of a dream."

A true-life case study by Rikki Hunt

The meat in an argument.

"I was around 21 when I became a store manager for Safeway food stores in Poole, Dorset. This was my first job as a manager.

The store had been open around seven years and had never made a profit. The bosses assumed that this was because of its location on the outside of a covered shopping complex.

I loved that store from the moment I entered it as its fifth manager. The store was around 20,000 square feet (6,096 square metres), which was significant for its time, and I guess because it was losing money my bosses thought it would be a good testing ground for a young manager like me—after all, it could not get any worse.

At the end of my first day, which I had spent observing the store, checking the accounts, talking to customers and staff, I gathered the managers of the departments together so that I could introduce them to how I wanted us as a team to work together from here on in.

The short meeting began with me explaining that each day, at a time to be agreed, I wished to tour each department with the section manager or, in their absence, the deputy. I explained the tour would be limited to 20 minutes so being on time and giving clear information was relevant.

I stated that I wanted to understand their plans for their department and get an insight into the challenges they faced in trying to deliver them. My goal was to see where I could help, if at all, and give them feedback on how I felt the department worked and looked, then from time to time I would add some input on how their section was performing financially, which had not happened in the past.

There were seven departments, and six of the managers were

very enthusiastic and offered to do all they could to make the store profitable.

One manager called Phil, of the fresh meat department, was notably silent during that meeting. Phil was in his early 40s, so twice my age, and I sensed that this mattered to him. I chose not to raise the issue of his silence in the meeting but instead moved on to offer each manager a 20-minute slot in my diary every day for the near future. After some interdepartmental negotiation six of these slots were taken up eagerly and you can guess who kept quiet throughout!

As he hadn't offered any opinion, I merely allocated the only available time slot to Phil and the meat department. Phil was unable to hold his anger or his tongue any longer and decided to tell me in front of all the others that "just because as part of my training I had completed an eight-week butchery course it did not make me a butcher". I ignored his anger and calmly said: "Phil, let's just do the tour and see what you think afterwards." Shortly after the discussion the meeting came to its natural end and he, along with the rest of us, left for the evening.

Next morning at the agreed (by me anyway) time I arrived in front of the meat department and could see through the glass window into the cutting area. Phil was making it obvious that he was busy and was not going to play.

I went back to the front of the store and picked up a customer shopping trolley and proceeded to amble along the meat counter trying to see the goods on display purely as a customer. I'd stop every now and then, picking up the odd piece of beef or some chops and putting the items into my trolley. While doing his best not to look, Phil could see what I was doing, and it eventually drove him mad. He came around to the customer side of the meat counter and demanded to know what I was doing. I told him I was taking off display those packs of meat that I did not think looked good to a customer and suspected that no one would buy.

He stared at me in disbelief, looked down into my trolley and then almost screamed at me: "They only need bloody re-wrapping", to which I of course calmly replied, "Phil, you are the master butcher here, if that is your professional assessment then only re-wrap them." I left him with the trolley and made my way to the next department.

It would have been effortless for me to have taken a different route with Phil. He had shouted at me and attempted to ridicule me in front of his peers. I could quickly have taken my cues from his emotional outbursts and ended up in arguments and conflict, and knowing Phil, all-out war. Instead, I chose to be patient, stand my ground, remain calm and demonstrate that I recognised his ability as a butcher. Each day at the appointed time I'd show up and conduct the same 'customer survey' and each day he would eventually come out and take the questionable items away. Sometimes I got a snotty reaction, sometimes an icy shoulder. I kept my focus—improve things for the customer and sales will go up, and remove anything that customers are not likely to appreciate.

I took what opportunities I could with him one-to-one, or during other management meetings, to convey that I wanted his ideas on how he could help improve customer satisfaction and sales. I asked for his input, in the same way I asked for every manager's input on how to tackle department performance issues. If we could turn a profit in any one department, then all the other departmental managers benefit, and if we could turn a profit across the whole store then we would all also benefit even more.

Once Phil realised I was not the wet nose he had initially thought, and I was not going to be drawn in or deflected by his emotional outburst he began to change. When he started to contribute positively then the real progress began to occur, and within only four months this deadbeat, forever loss-making store turned in its first month of profit. Only a small profit but a profit nonetheless, and every manager, including Phil, knew the future was going to be a lot brighter.

What did I learn about persuasion from that period of my life?

Firstly, that even when it is in someone's self-interest to agree with a proposal, it does not mean that they will. There are lots of reasons people turn down great opportunities, and that includes some reasons that do not make much sense on any level.

Secondly, when emotions are involved, the facts of the matter often fly out of the window. Being perceived as the young upstart who was going to tell someone how to do his job didn't help Phil and me get off to a great start. Arguing with him or putting him in his place through a disciplinary process was never going to turn things around. I had to stay calm and stay focussed because an argument would only serve to cement his belief and entrench his position. You can never honestly win an argument because, as someone much wiser than I am said: "Someone who is forced to change his view is of the same opinion still…"

Lastly, we sometimes persuade others more by our behaviour than our words. Stephen Covey once said: "You cannot talk yourself out of something you behaved yourself into." I stood up to Phil calmly. I kept my focus on improving things for the customer, something he could not really argue with. I kept showing him respect and asking for his input. Within weeks he came around and engaged fully with the process because I played it straight. No tricks, no techniques, no arm twisting and no bull."

Applications

Application example—John Fletcher—cycle tracks

Imagine this scenario:
John Fletcher was the assistant to the chief town planner in Devonshire County Council. He had recently joined the council from university and saw a career for himself in local government. John had a specific interest in Flavingham, as he grew up there. A small town under the council's authority, Flavingham has evolved beyond all predictions over the past 10 years with an influx of both young people and families. New, affordable housing has encouraged many people to move there from both London and the principal town of Plympton in the county.

John's aim:
John saw there was a distinct shortage of parks, recreational areas and, specifically, cycle tracks. In promoting the town's image and attracting further families with the prospect of a healthy lifestyle and an active family unit, John saw that the creation of 52 new cycle tracks covering 287 miles over the next five years would indeed provide the right facilities to meet the needs of this growing and changing community. This was quite a revolutionary idea as the town at that time had no cycle tracks, and there were no plans for them in the town's development plan and three-year budget. The town had excellent road links with many local attractions that encouraged many tourists and visitors to the area.

However, John believed that his idea would not only attract more visitors that the area needed but it would position the town as a much more attractive place for growing families to love.

John wasn't so sure that it would be easy to influence others to accept his idea.

Influencing challenge:

John reported to Peter Butterworth, the chief town planner, who was due to retire in three years' time. John hadn't mentioned his idea because he was unsure of how to pitch it, and he foresaw a few challenges:

1. Peter Butterworth cared very much about the community and was conscientious in providing the optimum range of services for its residents. Having said that, he had no wish to 'rock the boat' by recommending any radical new ideas with so little time left before his retirement. All he wanted to do was see out his remaining three years with stability by biding his time. Would he indeed welcome such a radical new idea that could have been perceived as causing him headaches and upheaval in the twilight years of his long service to the council? Probably not.
2. Peter Butterworth reported to Bill Staines who was the financial controller. Bill was quick to remind everyone that budgets were stretched as it was, and with no future provision for any cycle track, John's idea could well get knocked back as being unfeasible and a poor investment. What would it take for cycle tracks to be considered as worthy of allocating a budget over the next five years?
3. John was new to the council, and although he had a good working relationship with Peter Butterworth (his boss), he was relatively unknown to Bill Staines. Peter, on the other hand, had an excellent working relationship with Bill. If Both Peter and Bill liked the

idea, they could take it and propose it at the next Forward Planning Committee meeting of which they were both vital members. How could John get his voice heard with credibility?

What might be the best approach for John to take with this information to help influence the acceptance of his idea?

Possible influencing approach

The keys to John's success would lie in his planning, his research and the extent that he could use his excellent relationship with his boss, Peter Butterworth.

1. Planning and research

John needed to research quite carefully economic and demographic trends nationally (possibly globally) as well as locally. With the shape of the world changing, different work patterns were emerging, and lifestyles were changing. It was, therefore, necessary to research this area's past and current usage, as well as the projected future growth, to demonstrate demographic changes with younger families moving in with different needs.

John needed to extrapolate current data, figures and trends to form a clearer picture as to the community needs of Plympton, in, for example, 10 years' time.

John also needed to consider future costings for such a project along with an anticipated project plan. Costs would become a crucial issue when the final decision was discussed, so John needed to research the effectiveness of the use of current budgets by examining under/ or overspending.

What positive effects would cycle tracks have in the community? Would they allow sports and recreational activities to be more accessible? What potential returns could the local business community expect as benefits?

John also needed to prepare a 'what if?' list based on questions or concerns that would be most readily voiced by the Council as it moved further forward in the decision-making process. All these issues, and undoubtedly more, would need to be considered before he could come forward to initially voice his idea.

2. Presenting ideas to Peter Butterworth

John had a good working relationship with Peter which meant his proposal was likely to be heard more objectively and attentively than by approaching anyone else. Not only that, but Peter Butterworth had an excellent relationship with Bill Staines, and he had an intimate knowledge of how and when to present the idea to Bill—which assumed Peter was behind him, of course, in favour of his proposal. Although Peter was retiring in three years, he could position it so that John could earn 'brownie points' in his own career—if John sold the idea to him first. He would also have a better idea of the best way to move it forward to Bill Staines

Explaining to Peter that he could oversee the project with no hassle or stress for him, allowed Peter to see out the remaining three years with a degree of stability. At the same time, he would be able to continue delivering the optimum range of services to meet the future needs of Plympton's residents—a consideration that was particularly important to Peter.

John needed to prepare his case for the meeting with Peter for his initial pitch and be armed with:

- An explanation of the benefits a better use of facilities would provide with more spend for businesses

- A breakdown of the potential consequences long term if the council did not adopt his proposal
- A proposal for how the budget to create the cycle tracks could be covered: by a possible increase in council revenue from more visitors to the town; from funding taken from another area of the council's spending; or the possible creation of a new budget

If he were unable to make it clear to Peter how his idea would benefit the council or the community, it would be unlikely that John's proposal would go much further.

3. Work with Peter to present the idea to Bill Staines

Once John had achieved the first stage of influencing Peter to take the proposal on board and had obtained his agreement with his plan, Peter would require help and support from John when he presented it to Bill. John had to consider the following:

- Make sure he had all the information he required.
- Would Bill require that information in a specific format?
- What concerns did Peter have in meeting with Bill?
- What did Peter think were the possible concerns/questions that Bill was expected to raise?

Remember that Peter had an excellent relationship with Bill, so if Peter supported and even presented John's idea, it would look as if he had originated the plan, or at least had been involved in its development. Therefore the plan had to be seen as an idea that had merit and was therefore worthy of Bill's consideration.

Application example—June Bartlett—cupcakes

June Bartlett is very proud of her cakes, and so she should be because her home-based business attracts a great deal of praise from her many customers. When she started baking three years ago she only made her cakes for family and friends but now is in demand for birthdays, weddings, anniversaries, and even more sombre occasions. Most of the orders are small, for six to twelve cupcakes, but there is an ongoing request for many types of cupcakes for different events.

June's aim:
When June started making cupcakes three years ago, the process of buying materials, baking, producing and delivering the cakes was manageable despite her being on her own. However, as time has gone on and the orders have grown, it is proving increasingly difficult trying to meet deadlines and to fit other aspects of her life into every 24 hours. June has been thinking for some time about how to make the process more manageable, but recent events have focussed her mind on what she feels needs doing.

A thriving local company made a tentative enquiry to determine how well placed she is to produce a weekly supply of four varieties of her cakes, consisting of 100 of each type, for their staff canteen. 400 cupcakes a week! As it stands now, it is an impossible task. However, if she could convince the company that she is able to fulfil their requirement, it could lead to other orders from them and could well attract interest from further afield and from other businesses. This could allow her small business to grow into a more viable and profitable operation.

Influencing challenge
1. To fulfil such an order June would need new machinery to help automate part of the process, but she has no financial resources to meet the anticipated £500 costs. She also needs to employ someone part-time to assist her and will have to approach her bank for funding, even though she is a long-standing customer she has no real track record with them

as a business account. How can she approach the bank for financing with the prospect of potential business rather than firm agreements?
2. June is aware of the idea that going to the bank with a firm order will make her application for funding more attractive to the bank. She plans to approach her prospective client and persuade them to give her a trial order, which in turn will enable her to go to the bank with a firm order, rather than something speculative. But how can she influence the client that this is a safe option for them?
3. June has in mind Susan, a local neighbour (who she gets on well with and who always takes an active interest in June's cupcakes and is very complimentary about them wishing she were as capable as June). June considers that Susan, who seems to possess all the necessary skills and attributes, would be an ideal candidate to help her part-time. Susan, however, appears pre-occupied with school activities and other things involving friends. How could June influence Susan, with her busy lifestyle, that to help her make cupcakes part-time would be a good idea?

With three points of influencing to consider, what might be June's best start point, and what might be the best approach for her to take?

Possible influencing approach

It is assumed that June wants to expand the business, so the current development could be the catalyst for it to happen. June needs to address three areas: Susan her friend, the client, and the bank. She doubtless will want to consider the sequence of which steps to take and in which direction. It would seem logical that June should speak with Susan first; then to her client; then the bank. The thinking is that with more robust data, she can go to the bank with a detailed business plan.

Susan—June should start to consider what she thinks would be a good time to talk with Susan. After all, she has expressed interest before so it wouldn't seem out of place to initiate a conversation with her now. June could then ask some questions designed to uncover Susan's thoughts and feelings and where her aspirations may lie and how she might react to an opportunity to do something she enjoys.

- Does she like the cupcakes? What does she think about them?
- Would she like to be able to make them? Is it an interest she'd like to explore?
- Find out about whether she has the time available during her day to commit?

Once June has uncovered sufficient information she can then let Susan know about her plan and that she would like Susan to get involved and help. She can reinforce her idea by informing Susan that she thinks she has the skills and qualities to do the job. If Susan were to join June, it would really help them both. Susan would be able to make cupcakes for her family as well as June's customers, and with the extra production capacity June would earn more money. In other words, she can sell the idea to her after she discovers if Susan is ready to be sold to!

June also needs to make sure that by offering Susan the part-time role it doesn't have to conflict with her other day-to-day activities. Susan's work for June needs to be arranged for a time that suits Susan best.

June's client—After her discussion with Susan, June will then be able to arrange a meeting with her potential client.

This will offer the opportunity for her to clearly explain that she wants the order and is currently in the process of improving her procedures to deal with the demand and will soon be ideally placed to fulfil the client's order requirements.

June could ask for a trial order of either half or a proportion of the original amount that she could fulfil with Susan's help. By then the bank would have stepped in to help, or she could use the profits from the trial order to provide funding for some of the equipment she requires.

Bank—June would need to carefully prepare for a meeting with her bank manager. She would need to develop a detailed business plan that includes the growth of her business to date, along with confirmation of the trial order from the client, with a letter of intent for a more significant order, or orders, to follow.

June could also explain to the bank that with Susan onboard to support her, her business venture will be a relatively safe risk for the bank if it agrees to provide the finances she needs.

Application example—Maria Felsted—promotion

Maria Felsted works at Argo Pharmaceuticals, a global pharmaceuticals company in central France. She is a good, steady, reliable worker and has been with the firm 12 years. Maria initially started working in central operations, learning the ropes so to speak, and then spent four years on secondment in their Basle office.

Back at the company's headquarters in central France, Maria has been operations manager for France for the last nine months, a role in which she excels, although her inexperience was challenging in the first few months. However, Maria sees her future with Argo. She is single, flexible and adaptable. As a hard worker, she is viewed positively as a progressive steady member of the workforce who always delivers consistent results. Her boss is new to the company, but Maria has a reliable history with Argo and consistently scores highly in her annual appraisals and is proving to be a great support to her new boss.

Maria's aim:
Maria wants to progress and now has her eye on an opportunity for a future promotion. The company is undergoing a significant phase of growth through acquisition in North America and the far eastern markets. However, it is clear to Maria that operations have not yet developed its new markets, but with further new product launches planned for next year, the company is going to want to recruit a global operations manager to oversee the growth, a role Maria is well equipped to fulfil. She decides to apply for the new position once the opportunity arises.

In recent days, Maria has learned that the company is indeed planning to recruit a global operations manager and plans to advertise the position internally in the next few weeks. Maria wants to secure that job, so starts her thought process to prepare her application.

Influencing challenge
It may appear on the surface that Maria is an ideal candidate, as indeed she may well prove to be. However, there are some considerations the company could have that Maria will want to consider.

1. Her boss is new to the company, and she may feel she is better placed to succeed in this new role than Maria. Indeed, the company may think so too. What reasons can Maria give to show that she is better equipped than her new boss? Will this cause tension between them in the interim period?

2. She has only been in her current role for 9 months, which the company may feel is insufficient time to give her the necessary experience to take on a more significant role. Wouldn't the company feel she is better off staying where she is, where she can continue gaining experience for future opportunities which are bound to arise as the company continues to grow?
3. The company (while supportive) is aware of the extent that she struggled in the first few months of her present role. Couldn't the same be said if she were to step into the newly-created global role? Could the company accept her struggling in the way they did in her present role? How could she be sure she would cope if she were to be appointed to the new position?
4. The company may want to recruit an outsider rather than promoting from within, which has been their policy to date. It is possible that an outsider will bring broader experience with them from a previous position in such a role which could offer a more extensive base of lessons and skills to the company. That would be a fair thing for the company to consider, but in Maria's mind it doesn't mean she could not cope with doing the job.

How should Maria approach her application in a way that will help influence the company that (despite these potential concerns) she is the right person for the job?

Possible influencing approach

As in all influencing situations, nothing is guaranteed; so you should always try to maximise your level of influence in each case. Maria may well need to work hard at influencing the company to offer her the job, although firm commercial decisions such as recruiting an outsider may well swing the ruling against her. Having said that, there are several things Maria should do to persuade them in two key areas: preparation and execution.

1. Preparation

- Maria needs to be well prepared to manage the questions and concerns the company is likely to have when she makes her application. What lessons has she learned? Why does Maria think she is equipped to do the job after only 9 months in her present role? Why does she think she wouldn't struggle in the same way that she has before?
- She needs to research the market and global trends in the pharmaceutical industry to anticipate future operational needs and the resources required.
- She will need to update and tailor her résumé in line with the specification and position profile that is outlined in the internal advertisement.
- She will have to prepare her case to present herself most appropriately. For example, by highlighting the benefits to the company of recruiting internally. She should be prepared, of course, for the company to counter this by using their argument for recruiting externally, so she needs to be ready to respond accordingly.
- She will need to prepare a list of her achievements to date in the business and show how she has helped by contributing to the success of the company.
- She will need to demonstrate her operational efficiency in a measurable way.
- She will have to determine an action plan that will explain how she can make a success of the new role based on her

research and knowledge of the company and how it might achieve global operational excellence in the coming years.

2. The execution

Being well-prepared for the interview is vital, as is the need for Maria to project confidence in her ability to undertake this new role. At the same time, she must take care not to be perceived as either 'cocky' or overconfident.

It would be important for Maria to be regarded as being well prepared for the interview with answers to her interviewers' questions that provide solid reasons why she feels she is the right choice.

Maria needs to ensure that she is ready for any questions that can sometimes throw people. These might include:

- "Why should we employ you?"
- "What specifically can you bring to this role?"
- "What are the risks we are likely to face by offering you the role?"
- "What are your weaknesses? Or areas that you need to develop?"

Maria should be prepared and ready to handle these questions with calm confidence. She must also be prepared to answer any of the questions above and be capable of fielding any negative responses by referring to her action plan to achieve optimum global operational efficiency. Her plan may well offer ideas that other candidates may not have considered, especially if they do not have inside knowledge of the company.

If Maria can pre-empt well enough some of the questions and concerns that the company may have, such as her lack of experience, or how she struggled before, she should be able to address these concerns in a positive and pro-active way.

However, she needs to consider how she will feel if the company decides this move is not right for her at this specific time, and that commercially it would be more appropriate to recruit an outsider. As with all these things, preparation is key to helping Maria decide whether it is right for her to apply in the first place. If she believes it is appropriate for her to apply, she must be confident she can present a positive case for being considered the right person for the new role. This will include preparing well-thought-out reasons that include economic arguments to support her application capable of outweighing any questions or concerns her interviewers may have.

REFLECT AND LEARN

What ideas did you take from this chapter that were original, fresh, or new to you? What teaching was familiar? In what ways do you already apply some of this learning?

How did you react emotionally and cognitively to the ideas in this chapter? What concepts do you agree with and why? What do you disagree with and why?

What were the most exciting or useful insights gained from reading and thinking about this chapter?

In what ways might you translate the ideas presented throughout this chapter into practical, useful, everyday ideas and plans?

What new questions about persuasion do you now have after reading this chapter?

ACTION LEARNING

In addition to the three original examples you selected at the beginning of the book, list several other people that might benefit from what you have learned about persuasion.

Set yourself some time-phased goals to apply what you have learned that you listed in the Reflect and Learn section; some goals to guide your actions over the next three months, the next three weeks and the next three days.

Thinking about how you plan to apply your learning, what obstacles might you encounter along the way? And, realistically, how might you deal with them?

Who else could you share these ideas with as a supportive sounding board or informal coach? How might you go about setting up a conversation with them to enrol them in supporting your application of this teaching? What might be some of the reasons that would persuade them to become involved? How might they also benefit?

7

The Summary

Summary

This book has been entirely about encouraging you to think about how you might best go about persuading another person. But, here's a question to consider: has anyone tried to persuade **YOU** to do something recently?

Of course they have; as recently as in the past few days I'd hazard a guess! Before that, it was probably the day before that, and the day before that too. What is the message?

The message is that the act of persuasion is happening all the time, right across the world, every day. Anyone who considers he/she doesn't need to persuade (or won't admit to ever having been persuaded!) doesn't exist. An individual might say that it isn't my job to persuade somebody else to do something. They may add that it just "isn't my personality to persuade others". If they refuse to accept that persuasion in one form or another has never featured in their lives, then they are probably in denial and kidding themselves about other matters too.

The need to persuade someone somewhere for something is fundamental to life; it is woven into the fabric of our entire makeup as well as within the society we live in. Nobody is exempt from the art of persuasion—that, of course, includes you, me, and everybody else on the planet for that matter.

Persuasion happens all the time, every day, and affects everybody in some shape or form. In its most subtle way, it can be cunning, deceitful, sometimes undetectable—nevertheless, persuasion is there, somewhere, lurking in the shadows. We have seen that from the moment a baby is born, the offspring will cry to persuade his or her mother to give them milk. A baby cries when it is hungry, needs its nappy changed, when it is ill or just to say it needs comforting. Every one of these acts is a form of persuasion—devised to get their own way. This process—that people are either always *being persuaded* or trying *to persuade* others.

Thinking back to the last person who tried to persuade you, have you ever considered how they went about it?

"In making a speech one must study three points. First, the means of producing persuasion; second, the language; and third, the proper arrangement of the various parts of the speech." (Aristotle)

More importantly, were they successful? If they were, then how did they achieve this? Conversely, if they were not successful, why did they not succeed in persuading you? Questions like this will help consider the process and shape your understanding of how others think when attempting to persuade you, and the extent to which they considered you and your needs in the process.

What has history told us?

We know that Greek philosophers taught us much about successful persuasion. The myth that to be successful at persuading others by merely offering a logical argument and resting on the strength of the points you raised in it are folly and were destroyed by the likes of Socrates, Plato and Aristotle. Again, it comes back to one of the central themes of this book; notably, that the persuader must not only pursue an understanding of the other person they are trying to persuade, but they must establish emotional connections at the same time as a base for their argument to sit on.

We have read how William Wilberforce led the Committee for the Abolition of the Slave Trade. Formed in 1787, this eventually led to the convincing movement that finally encouraged the passing of the Great Reform Act in 1832. Let us not forget Columbus and his art of persuading a King and Queen in April 1492 to sign a contract guaranteeing him all that he desired in his attempt to find a shorter route to Asia.

We told the story of how in more recent years Peter Marsh, head of the advertising agency Allen, Brady & Marsh (ABM), and his brave, and some might say audacious presentation, managed to persuade Peter Parker of British Rail to hand him the company's advertising account.

There are so many other examples that litter history extending back to the beginning of time, but, conversely, may have happened this very morning. The need for one individual to persuade another really does reach as far back as the beginning of mankind when, in the Garden of Eden, Eve was alleged to have persuaded Adam to take a bite from the apple. So, what has history told us? Foremost, in the context of this book, it has informed us that thorough research, planning and understanding of the other person, and tapping into their needs and motivations, are the vital keys that so often unlock the door of persuasion. If someone has already invented the wheel—why reinvent it? Is today any different? Other than the fact that each situation is unique and is acted out by different people at different times, the same sense of persuasion continues to challenge us.

So why DO we need good persuasive skills?

At the very beginning of this book you may recall we posted this question—**'Why would you want to persuade anyone about anything?'** Well, now you have had the chance to ponder and consider what your answer will be to that question because you are in a position to understand that we all persuade someone about something all the time.

Persuasion itself—what's it all about? Well, Persuasion is not a process of arguing, putting your point of view, voicing your opinion or talking someone down. Persuasion, as we have shown, is primarily about doing three essential things, and doing them well.

1. **Connect with the person**—No doubt you have heard the expression—'open mouth and insert foot'? Lack of thought and planning about what you want to say to someone is undoubtedly a key factor to why many people fail to persuade in the way they'd like to. "I didn't mean it to come across like that" is often repeated in conversations. Or another example: "I didn't mean to offend you". These demonstrate just how people often open their mouths without first engaging their brains. Before you speak, you must always think through how you will connect meaningfully with the other person without causing them any offence.
    Some thought in advance about:
    a) The person
    b) The situation
    c) The message you wish to convey and where the other person currently sits on the points you want to persuade them on
    d) The possible, likely questions, or concerns, the other

person may have to your approach are all considerations that lead to a successful act of persuasion
e) When you get the basics right, it can bring many worthwhile benefits that will help you with the persuasion process
2. **Appealing to the other person's heart**—It is so easy to want to force our logic on people because we feel our points have merit and should be listened to. Appeal to the person about what interests them, rather than appeal to them to listen to your points of view and opinions. What is it that motivates that person? What are they interested in? What is it they want more of—or less of?

> *"Talk to someone about themselves,*
> *and they'll listen for hours."*
>
> —Dale Carnegie,
> *How to Win Friends and Influence People*

3. **Make your case appealing**—Position your logic in such a way that—to the person you are reaching out to—your motives are exciting and that you make perfect sense to them. Of course, you can only do that if you understand the other person. Frame the elements of your proposal in a 'benefit format' with a suggested course of action.

Persuading today

The PERSUADE model we have looked at is a highly adaptable and flexible sequential model. Most situations where there is an element of persuasion will almost certainly use some, if not all, of the aspects of **P.E.R.S.U.A.D.E.** Each case is, by its very nature, situational. So, in some cases, it may take months to complete every element, while other aspects may take mere minutes as a thought process. We've looked at other factors and other tools we may choose to use, depending on the situation and the result we are looking for.

How does the future look for Persuasion?

What do we know about the future? What does anyone know about the future? Well, we are aware it is continually evolving. The sheer pace of change within our society over the last 25 years has been considerably quicker than during the previous decade and a half. Nowhere are changes more prevalent and apparent than in the media. Today we have a plethora of media available, all being used tactically to ensure that advertiser's messages and unique selling propositions (USPs) reach their 'target market' to try and persuade you to buy this, trial that offer, support this cause, etc, etc—the list is endless!

Advertising is moving more towards digital and away from print and that move opens a myriad of potential channels of persuasion due to the sheer versatility of the internet. It is not just the number of social networking sites available, but the way an individual's messages can reach their target audience. The plethora of devices available now includes iphones, ipads, laptops, tablets, watches, Google Glass and Virtual Reality Headsets, to name a few digital gadgets. The format you can use is diverse, and seldom does a day pass without another invention coming onto the market that we can interact with. We have email, SMS text, eshots, plus of course the more traditional forms of mediums that use persuasion.

Where do people go to send messages? Again, we are spoilt for choice. We have platforms such as Facebook, LinkedIn, WhatsApp and Twitter and a plethora of other social networking sites. None of these existed prior to 1997 (Six Degrees is often cited as the first recognisable Social Media Platform) so who knows what will appear and be the latest sensation during the next decade? Traditional forms of advertising have or are being replaced by others. Different methods are being employed to persuade people; different avenues and media are being developed; new tactics are being deployed. Some of these are very subtle; others are brutal, often projecting shocking imagery; and charity appeals that pull at our heartstrings by stirring emotions to persuade us to donate money. Some forms of persuasion used in the media are more successful than others—'different strokes for different folks' as they say.

So, things change as they always will, apart from one thing: persuasion! People will still allow themselves to be persuaded, to stop doing something, start doing something, think something, or do something differently and so on! We could say that whether we are the one doing the persuading—or being persuaded—we are all vulnerable to the 'power of persuasion'.

In your job at work, you may not be employed in sales or marketing; you may not have cause to stand up to deliver persuasive presentations to groups; you may not be required to be that gregarious person, that social animal that seems to work better through people than others do. However, this does not mean we are not involved in the act of persuasion in all walks of our lives. Neither does it mean that we don't need to persuade because we do! We all need to persuade someone to do something almost every single day. The fact is, we have become so conditioned to persuasion that we tend to take it for granted, so that we are frequently unaware that we are either being persuaded—or engaging in the act of persuasion!

Increasing your ability to persuade will not only help you to become more confident in yourself but will also help you to build stable, long-term relationships with others. It will also help you create new and increased opportunities and go some way towards making you happier with the results you achieve for your efforts.

So, how is all this going to help you? Having the ability to efficiently persuade others will assist you to become more productive in whatever occupation you are in. It will help you maximise your productivity and achieve your goals. If you are not interested in doing this, then why otherwise would you be reading this book?

The next time you want to persuade someone, remember this…

The good news in all that you have just read is that what you have learned from the exercise should now prove to you that you are in control of what you do in your approach to persuading others. You can step back and think through all the elements in this book, maybe using the **P.E.R.S.U.A.D.E.** model to gauge the best method to use when approaching another person. You can choose—you have choices. There seem to be very few things more liberating in life than having the freedom to choose. Remember that in some regimes, citizens are frequently denied this freedom, so we should be thankful that we have this facility.

Of course, life's best lessons are learned by 'doing' and 'experiencing'. So, if one style or approach doesn't appear to bring you the results you desire, try another. People will always need to be persuaded; like a missed bus, there will be another one along in a minute—it is the same with persuasion. If you lose your opportunity the first time, next time, by attempting a different approach, you may find that it works to your advantage.

Tomorrow there will always be someone that you will wish to persuade; and now—you can do it just that little bit better, can't you?

3